A New Heart: My Story of Abortion, Addiction and Conversion

Shawna Arnold

*A New Heart: My Story of Abortion,
Addiction and Conversion*

Shawna Arnold

© Shawna Arnold 2021

All rights reserved. Except for quotations, no part of this book may be reproduced or transmitted in any form or by any means, electronic or mechanical, including photocopying, recording, uploading to the internet, or by any information storage and retrieval system, without written permission from the publisher.

Published by Parousia Media Pty Ltd
PO Box 59
Galston, New South Wales, 2159
www.parousiamedia.com

Printed in Australia
ISBN: 978-0-6450907-7-2

Contents

An Abusive Childhood   9

Abortion and its Aftermath   31

Hope and Healing... and A New Life Begins   45

Reflections and Prayers   73

An Abusive Childhood

I grew up in a small town in Saskatchewan. The memories of my childhood could be described as chaotic, stressful and disappointing. I suffered from a lot of emotional, mental, and sexual abuse. This account jumps around a bit as many of my memories are vague and difficult. Extremely traumatic events have left my memories in pieces.

I was the oldest of three children, and my mother was very ill-equipped to deal with a colicky baby when I arrived. She would leave me in a room with a bottle and sleep away large parts of the day. In her inability to cope, she used to drop me off at my grandmother's house on a regular basis. Over time, I saw my grandmother as my 'rescuer', the one person I knew I could go to who would show me the love I desired and needed. However, as much as I loved being there, this was not a perfect situation either. My grandmother had eight children of her own, so having me around created a lot of envy and anger from some of my aunts. I was a bother, "Why don't you go home? You are always here."

I didn't care. Feeling at 'home' with grandma was always worth it. My grandma had a gentleness that attracted me to her. My grandma always had homemade remedies that would relieve my constant ear infections. I needed stability in my life, and she was the only person around me who stayed calm while enduring trials. I have never known her to show anger or hostility in any way.

My grandfather, on the other hand, was a very angry man. He was a war veteran, and I see now why he had so much anger and bitterness inside of him. The post-war trauma and hurt he obviously suffered was pointed towards my mum and then to me. The saying is true that hurting people hurt others. He used to call me names like "thing" and "it" along with other insults. I was always in trouble for leaving the lights on too long or for having the fridge door open for longer than ten seconds. The anger just built up inside him, and soon I could read his body language. I learned to be cautious around him and knew his triggers. When grandpa's anger was unavoidable, I would hide between my grandma and the cupboard she was leaning on to find shelter. I knew she would tell him to stop. I preferred this to the instability of my own home.

My parents were known for their fighting, and the whole family labelled them as the problem ones. My mother was a stay-at-home mum who was addicted to prescription pills. She had a profound spending habit, which meant my dad not only had a full-time job, but a few other jobs on the side.

My dad was what I call a 'ghost dad'. In the little time he spent at home, he never did much with us, and if he did, it was done very impatiently. He was always in a rush and seemed to panic a lot. Spending time with my dad meant going with him to his night jobs occasionally, because my mum would be at bingo and there was no one else to watch us that day.

I remember him being ashamed of his side jobs and of being talked about by the people in town. My dad worried about what other people thought about him. We would have to wait to leave his bank cleaning job until all the traffic was gone from Main Street then bolt out the door. He felt degraded for having to take on a second job as a janitor after working all day at his regular well-paid professional job.

Now, as an adult looking back, I realise he was a hurting man. But back then, as a young girl, I was just scared of my dad. He had a temper and for some reason I was his scapegoat. He used to spank me quite hard, and I remember how his face looked as he did it. He was filled with rage about a lot of things and spanking me seemed to release his anger.

When I was about four, my younger brother and I played with my mother's eyeglasses while she slept the morning away, and then we broke them. I knew that dad would be angry about the money to fix them. I got my brother dressed, put him in his wagon, and pulled him across town. When we got to the train tracks I couldn't get the wagon over the tracks, so I just carried my brother the rest of the way to my grandmother's and hid in the closet.

Back then people didn't lock their doors like they do now. For some reason, I felt safe hiding at my grandma's house. When my grandparents came home, they heard voices in their closet, and there we were. I remember being afraid of the spanking I would receive.

Another memory that sticks with me is the time my mother smashed my father's car by banging into it repeatedly with her car because he was at a meeting and she couldn't go to bingo. My brother and I were in the car, and I still remember the crashing sounds and jolts – and the terrifying fighting after that incident.

Soon it was time for me to start school. Having been from a Catholic background, it was only right to be placed in that school system. School seemed fine at first, a place that was predictable and regular. That changed as I got older. My grades were barely passing and no one would help me with my homework. The constant stress certainly contributed to my lack of success.

My mum had her third child now, so I had a second brother. I would go home for lunch and face the chaos that I was leaving my younger siblings to endure. One time on a lunch visit, I saw my two-year-old baby brother's hands were burnt and full of blisters. I was so angry! My mother had slept until noon again and my brother had somehow gotten hurt. I remember having so much anger towards her for being the way she was. Her routine was sleep until noon, go for coffee, make supper, and rush to bingo by six at night. This not only meant we took care of ourselves a great amount of the time, but it also meant we were left in the care of my grandfather while my mother and grandma would go to bingo together.

We would have to sit still while grandfather watched Matlock and Macgyver. We basically couldn't make any noise or the metre stick would come out. He used to chase me with the metre stick. As the oldest, I was the one punished if my brothers and I didn't behave. I remember where he kept that stick and knew when he would walk into the pantry he was coming out with that stick.

My mum would pick us up very late at night; we would be so tired, and I had school early in the morning. My father worked until late and so provided little relief from this routine.

When I would get home from school, I would be locked out because my mum was at coffee, so I had my usual back up plan of climbing through the kitchen window. If that didn't work, I would just have to hope that if I walked all the way to my grandparents' house someone would be home. This might not be such a big deal on a warm, sunny day, but we lived in Canada and the winter months were brutal.

All this stress obviously took its toll as I struggled to outgrow wetting the bed. I had painful and embarrassing rashes from the bed-wetting, and would tell my grandma who gave me corn starch to help sooth it. Staying overnight anywhere meant placing a towel under me; not much fun for sleep-overs. Mostly I stayed at my grandmother's for overnights, and I did that quite a bit. I felt like my grandma was all I had in life. All of my self-worth and security revolved around her. She was my safe place.

My dad would work long hours to cover the tab of my mum's spending habits. Work was also an escape from the reality of his life. We would see him for lunch; he would come home at noon, and then we wouldn't see him again until ten or eleven at night. At lunch, mum and dad would fight terribly and I would quickly eat whatever was easy to grab and run out the door. Lunch was never ready for us when we came home at noon. My mother would still be in bed or sitting on the bed partially dressed smoking a cigarette.

All morning my youngest brother would tend to his own needs and entertainment. I relived my own toddler years watching him, and it frustrated me to see him experience the same things. When

I returned to school, he stayed on my mind, wondering if he would be okay or if he would feel alone.

My mother had a serious mental illness and my dad would avoid us all by working non-stop. This soon would play a huge part in my development and the choices I would make as a pre-teen, and into adulthood.

I used to call the free offer ads as a child and bring home animals. I thought that I could receive love from animals, love that I was craving. I soon realised that I was not capable of providing for the animals I had so I would have to find them new homes. I guess I just craved something to hug. As a child I thought an animal could give me the love I needed.

I remember the anger my brother had at a young age and how he killed birds once. He took a baseball bat to the bird house outside and knocked it off the fence post. There were dead birds scattered on the lawn. At the time I thought he was just cruel, but now that I look back at the situation, that was how he dealt with his hurts in our family.

My mother would tell us to throw old food over the fence of our neighbours' home, and we would do it. My brother adopted a disrespect for other people, thinking it was hilarious especially if our mother was laughing and happy. It was good to see her happy sometimes even if we knew what we were doing was wrong.

My home was very dirty and I was embarrassed to bring friends over because of it. My mum hoarded clothes to the point that they rode up the walls in her bedroom. There were clothes with tags on that were never even worn but just thrown in the pile. I remember as a young girl sometimes cleaning the house for my mum to make her happy and getting some recognition from my dad for the effort. Maybe that is why I am a neat and tidy person now because of the shame I felt for my home being dirty as a child.

My mother continued to become more and more depressed and her actions were quite hurtful towards me. She would say dirty remarks to me that would insult my developing body as I became a teen. Ashamed of my body, I began wearing baggy clothes. When I would go over to my friend's house, my mother would tell my brother to mess up my room. I guess this was a way to punish me for not wanting to be home. I would come home to ripped posters and personal keepsakes scattered all over my room. I really hated her at the time, and I told her so to her face.

Despite our Catholic identity, she had the habit of consulting psychics and would purchase crazy potions through the mail. As a kid, I would sense things in the house especially when I was alone. It was a perfect breeding ground for infestations of evil. I used to tell my mum the strange things that would happen or I would see in the house, and she would throw holy water on me and tell me I was possessed. I sensed the evil in our home and was laughed at or ignored when I spoke of these occurrences. I eventually began keeping these things to myself because no one believed me. Besides, most people would consider me crazy for this sort of thing.

Stealing then became my mum's newest habit. Maybe she figured, 'If I can't buy it with money, I could still have it if I steal it'. Or maybe it was just a thrill to fill the emptiness. She would steal things from town and bring them home and tell us how easy it was to take them. I will never forget the time we went to the city, and my mum was charged with theft. We were stealing from a drug store and were spotted by an undercover surveillance officer. Once we exited the store, my mum was grabbed; my brothers and I stood paralysed with fear. I ran to a restroom to throw out the gum I had stolen because I didn't want to go to jail too. My parents fought a lot, but the argument that took place that night was terrifying for me to witness. Despite the terror of it all, shoplifting eventually became one of my own habits.

In my case, the old saying was right: like mother like daughter. At first I would steal money and small items from my friends' houses. Eventually this led to theft in stores. My mum laughed about the candy and toys I took, like it was a joke. My brother and I would also dress up in our uniforms from Brownies and Beavers and collect bottles. The cash was then used for candy. We were taught how to scam and get what we wanted despite how it might affect other people. Deep inside, I knew this was not only wrong but bizarre. I still kept doing it because my mum got a kick out of it.

Christmas time was usually a time we were showered with outrageous amounts of gifts when we were young children. As we got older, I never had Christmas with my family. In fact, I have never celebrated Christmas with my parents other than when I was young. I believe when we were young that was my mum's way of showing us love. Buying things for me was a way to ease her guilty conscience about how she treated me. My dad would be angry because once again the spending was an abuse of his hard-earned wages.

When I was about fourteen years old, my grandmother was diagnosed with emphysema. Her oxygen tank went everywhere with her. I always worried that the hose would come undone, and she would die because she wouldn't be able to breathe. I had to face the reality that life isn't forever, and that I could find myself alone, without my grandmother's protective presence. It was all too much for me and in a new world of teenage life and opportunities; avoiding the situation was the best I could do. I didn't really mean to abandon my grandma or to be ungrateful for the security she had provided me. I lived in a world of escape and had been carefully raised to find escape routes, and that is exactly what I did with her during this time.

There were constant doubts in my mind about any one I might attach myself to. My mum would tell me how my father hated me, and that he hated me because I was a woman. I was even told by my mum that my dad wasn't my biological father.

These lies made a home in my heart, and I would disrespect my dad and would call him names.

I was angry at my dad for never standing up to my mum and not understanding the hurt I was going through. It was easier as a child to lash out because that is how I learned to deal with my hurts. I wanted control of my life and thought that meant doing whatever I wanted.

I continued to be teased and ridiculed at school so when I had to transfer to a new school for fifth grade, I was glad. I thought I could possibly meet new friends. I met one girl, and we became best friends instantly. There were some problems in her home but not to the extent of mine. I spent a lot of time at her house and wouldn't come home much at all. My parents never came to get me, which made me feel I could do what I pleased. I never had a curfew because there was never any real discipline ever shown to me. My friend and I started to become interested in boys, and I remember us calling them and even meeting with some at her house.

I was filled with anger and shame at a very young age and was angry at God for the life I had. I remember throwing the Confirmation plaque and bending it because I was so mad at God. I couldn't understand as a child why God would allow so much to happen to me – an innocent child. I would even ask Him to kill me because I hated myself and my life. I eventually embraced and nurtured the deep anger and bitterness that was making a home in my heart.

As a very young child, I know I was touched inappropriately. I have blocked out most of the incidents, but do remember being in my room and the moon shining through the window and someone rubbing their genitals against me, maybe my babysitter. I have blocked many of the details out. My mother did nothing when I told her, leaving me to feel even more devalued and vulnerable.

There are other incidents of sexual abuse I recall, but I only remember bits and pieces. I was good at blocking out things that were painful for me. When I got older, I found new and better ways to block out the pain with sexual relationships and self-medicating.

I became promiscuous at an early age. I was awakened to sexual realities early in life and now realised I could get attention from men and that was what I wanted. I wanted to be acknowledged and loved. I lost my virginity very early to a man who was over 18. All I remember was being used and pretty much discarded afterwards. It was painful both physically and mentally, and really scarred my heart. The love I thought I would receive from him afterwards was not there, and the shame of the situation caused me to feel worthless and unwanted. I began to do other things to men for their pleasure, but I would not have intercourse with them. I never wanted to go through that pain again, yet I still caused pain to myself emotionally by letting myself be used.

I recall being at a party and drinking to the point I passed out and waking up with my pants unzipped and two guys lying beside me. I do not even know what they did to me. I had to get up and just brush it off like nothing happened. Rumours would circulate in the school about me, and I soon found myself hanging out with the so-called troubled kids in my town. They had similar problems in their lives and could relate to me to some degree. I soon began to drink, which then led to drugs. I thought I had found the answer I was looking for. I could numb my pain and not have to deal with my feelings. This was a lot easier than having to face the shame and hatred I had growing in my heart. I started using alcohol and drugs more often and would party at different places. A lot of the times, my friends and I would hang out with older guys who had their own places. They usually always had drugs and alcohol on hand. I started to basically sleep wherever I would pass out. I could act like a different person when I was using and say things I normally wouldn't say. It gave me an artificial sense of temporary self-esteem.

I remember coming home one day and finding out that my mum had packed up and left my dad, taking my youngest brother with her. It hurt me because I never knew anything about her leaving. I didn't even know where she had gone. I had to get that information from my grandparents.

My mum wouldn't allow me to live with her, so I ended up living with my dad and my other brother. I felt as though she had abandoned me: I was unwanted by my own mother. And despite the fact that I lived with my father, he wasn't there. He left for work at seven in the morning, just about the time I was coming home from a night of partying, ready to go to bed. At this late stage in the game, he had little to say. He was suffering with a divorce and a daughter who was killing herself slowly. He had no idea how to fix any of it, and his silence was proof of that. He never did spend much time with me to begin with, so it wasn't unusual that there was no communication between us.

My mum told me that the only reason he let me live there for that short time was because he didn't want to have to pay her child support.

Neither of my parents wanted me and that only contributed to my trying to find love in other places. I wanted to believe that I was lovable.

I had learned to be selfish, to run away from discomfort as best I could, so I had avoided the discomfort of watching my grandmother suffer. I'll never forget the day I was listening to 'Stairway to Heaven' and had just finished smoking a joint when my dad came into my room. He made a comment about the smell and then told me that my grandma had died. My grandma was sixty-three when she died of lung cancer. She had spent quite a bit of time in hospital before her death. I had quit spending time with my grandma because of my lifestyle. Maybe I thought it would be easier to separate from her than to see her suffer and die. It had been painful to watch her have trouble breathing and spit up mucus continually. This was the first time I had ever lost someone so close to me, someone I loved like a mother. After her death, I felt as though I had no one I could confide in anymore, no one I could truly trust.

I eventually got the nerve and went to see the school counsellor about what was going on in my life. To this day, I can't remember what I confided to her, but I do know that I was lost and needed to grieve my grandmother's death. With the help of that counsellor, I ended up living with the aunt and uncle who used to take me on camping trips.

I started to attend school regularly again and really was trying to pull myself together. It made me feel uncomfortable though to play the role of daughter to my aunt and uncle. My mind would wander to thoughts about my broken home, and I missed my brothers and grandma.

Things were going alright, and I tried to straighten myself out, but for some reason, I kept slipping and slipping. For many different reasons and in all the dysfunction, I left my aunt and went back to my mum.

I begged my mum to allow me to stay with her. It was what I was used to, but I also feared my mum would hurt herself now that my grandma was gone. I feared my mum would commit suicide because she had threatened it in the past. I worried about my brothers and how they were doing. As an adult looking back at the situation, I knew my aunt and uncle were doing what they thought was right in their hearts, and I appreciate them for doing so. My aunt told me that she prayed for me, and I know now that prayer is powerful.

Back in my chaotic life, I started cutting class and eventually just dropped out of school. The name calling by my peers at school was very hard for me to deal with. No one knew what I was going through. But at the same time, I didn't seem to care. I was an easy target for bullying. It is as though, when you are abused, people can smell you coming a mile away and will walk all over you to make themselves feel better. I couldn't handle the constant torment. I always feared the bell because I would be called terrible names by my peers as I went to my next class. At the time, with everything else I was going through, quitting school seemed the best option.

I started to get into trouble with the law and would steal to feed my addictions. I didn't care if I got caught. I just needed money to feed my addictions. I had enough charges against me that I ended up being sentenced to juvenile jail in Saskatoon. The charges I had then were theft over $1000, forgery and taking a motor vehicle without consent. My friend and I had stolen her mum's car and taken it on a joyride many miles away. We got stuck in a field after having a few drinks and had to walk to get help. The other guys in the car wouldn't walk so we set out to get help. I remember it was winter and extremely cold, and we started getting tired. I told my friend to stay awake and keep going. We finally saw a farm light and went to the house. We rang the doorbell. Fortunately it was a doctor who answered the door as we were suffering from hypothermia. I believe we would have died if this man had not been home.

I was sentenced to three months in jail, but was released early. I was then placed in a home with an elderly lady who was almost like an adoptive grandmother. She was very nice and would allow me to watch cartoons, and cook in her home. I felt a real loneliness inside my heart while I was in custody, but I believe it was just the feelings I had stuffed inside trying to surface. Since I wasn't drinking these feelings were not getting numbed.

While I was in jail, my mum was also doing community service back home for some of her own convictions. She had been placed on electronic monitoring and eventually served weekends in a women's jail. While there, she was found on the bathroom floor having tried to commit suicide.

Mum was severely depressed. As children, we didn't know how to deal with her illness. In fact I didn't even realise she had a mental illness until I was an adult. When you grow up seeing that all your life, you do not realise anything is wrong. It seems normal.

Once I was released on probation, I came back to my mum's house. I still partied, but I made sure I was home for my curfew, most of the time. I did not want to go back to jail and lose my freedom. Yet I still found creative ways to feed my addictions without getting caught. My friend would come on to older guys who were happy to get both of us drunk and high. I wasn't attracted to these men myself but knew they had money. My friend would repay them with sex, which I wasn't willing to do.

Meanwhile, my mum met a man who was soon to become my step-dad. He was a very large manic depressive. He beat her, and she would lie to me as to where her bruises were coming from. The bruises she showed me one time were horrific; I was told a bizarre story of how she had been raped by a cop and that was why she couldn't report it. This bothered me terribly, but I was so messed up myself; it just made me sink more into depression.

I kept doing drugs and drinking and eventually I was placed in another juvenile jail. My charges this time were failing to comply with a probation order, theft under $1000, five counts of forgery, and mischief under $1000. The police shackled me up, and my friend as well, and flew us to Regina Juvenile Detention Centre. Oddly enough I was excited about my first experience in a plane, but I was still scared of the different people being transported. I really didn't mind Regina. You were fed regularly and would go on trips and outings together as a group from time to time. I missed my brothers, and I wanted my freedom back, but there were good moments there. This one youth worker played catch with me in the backyard, and tried to encourage me by telling me I had a good arm. I felt uncomfortable though because I never knew how to accept compliments; I was more used to ridicule and criticism.

My mum never visited. She always had excuses like having no money for gas and things like that. When I was released, I would just sleep wherever I had passed out the night before at home. I never had a bedroom that was mine. It depended on where we were living and how many bedrooms the place had. My mum seemed to get evicted from every place she stayed; she must have moved a dozen times in the small town we were from.

The rent wasn't the first bill to be paid, neither was food. I even recall stealing food from parties because we had none at home. If we did have food, I wasn't allowed to eat it. If I had food, I would eat so fast that one of my friend's used to ask me if I breathed when I would eat. My step-dad had put a lock on the deep freeze, not allowing my mum to feed me, and my brothers weren't eating much either. It had to be by God's hand that we survived without becoming ill from malnutrition. The money I would steal would help me to eat things that were convenient and cheap, like fries and gravy, chips, Chinese food.

My mum and my step-dad did things to me that really hurt me deeply. I recall going to the local video store and being told I couldn't rent movies because I owed them money. Apparently they had taken out movies in my name and never returned them. There was also a time when I was given a large cheque from the government because my mum was on disability and she somehow was able to cash it and took most of the money. The only reason she gave me some of the money was so I wouldn't charge her for fraud. They even had credit cards out in my little brother's name. He learned about this later when he became an adult and had a bad credit history.

The way I felt for my mum back then was pure hate and anger due to the things she would do to her own children. I made a vow in my heart that I would never be the kind of mother who could hurt her kids. These were my feelings at this time in my life and the anger just grew inside of me. My younger brother was covered in bruises one day, all the way up and down his legs and body. I knew my step-dad had hit him. My first reaction was anger towards my brother for not telling me, and then I turned my anger towards my step-dad and told him I would kill him, if he ever hit my brother again.

My brother told me later in life, that I had also thrown my step-dad out of the house that day and I can't even remember doing that. The rage I had inside of me was scary. My brother told me that after that day my step-dad never hit him again. I am unsure if he hit my mum anymore after that; only she would know. That was the second time I had thrown him out, a man who was 6'4", and well over 200 pounds. I had thought I had gotten rid of him, but my mother just kept letting him back in. I couldn't be a constant guard dog, even though this killed me inside.

I soon started to get into heavier drugs and would be using mushrooms, acid, weed, hash, and I even crushed up pills and snorted them to get high. I was now living for drugs and alcohol. I would do anything for them, and they came before anyone else in my life. Drugs and alcohol seemed to mask the pain I had inside me. I couldn't approach a man without being drunk and high. My self-esteem was terrible.

I couldn't even look anyone in the eye. I trusted no one. One time, I remember just taking off with one of my friends and her boyfriend and we drove to Ontario. Who knows what I thought I would do there? She had money and a lot of weed so we would smoke the whole way there and sleep in hotel rooms along the way. One night her boyfriend made a pass at me so I told her. He threatened to beat me up and said I was lying. I knew I had to go home because she wasn't going to side with me over him. I found a church in Ontario where the pastor gave me money for a bus ticket home. He and his wife were so nice to me – they even gave me money for food at the bus depot. I have always been grateful to them in my heart for helping me get home.

When I got home my mum said, "Why did you come back?" Even though I should have known this would be the response, I was crushed. I felt so unwanted, and I had absolutely no respect for who I was at that time.

People do really strange things when they are hurting and wounded. We all tend to react differently to pain. Having grown up this way, and reflecting on my reactions to hurt in my life, I have, as an adult, become more compassionate and understanding to others.

Abortion and its Aftermath

I had missed my period and had a small bulge in my abdomen. With the continued drugs and partying, I became pregnant when I was nineteen years old. I told my mum who advised me to have an abortion. I was so messed up at the time that I believed the people who said there was no way I could take care of a baby. The doctor told me the baby was the size of a pen dot, had no heartbeat and wasn't even recognisable as a person. With my appointment to have the abortion in Saskatoon, I left the clinic. I kept drinking, and I even did some drugs, despite knowing I was pregnant. I remember my friend telling me she would help me raise this baby, but she was more messed up than I was at the time. Another girl I knew told me it was my body, my choice. I was confused and had no real support to turn to. My dad wasn't in my life and, quite frankly, it didn't seem like he cared any way. So I had nowhere to turn. I was completely lost and frightened.

I had no strength inside me to quit my addictions, and I chose them over my own baby's life. I was on mushrooms when I was pregnant and had thoughts that I had Satan in my stomach – that my baby was evil. I was a serious mess and needed help, some kind of treatment. I didn't even know who was the father of the baby I was carrying. It was between two guys that I had been seeing at the same time.

Well the day came for me to have my abortion, and I was driven to the hospital in the city by my friend along with the man from whom we scammed money. I don't even know if he knew why we were going to the hospital in the first place. My friend left me there, telling me she would come back to get me when I was done. I was all alone in the hospital and scared.

I was sedated so that I slept through the entire procedure. I remember waking up and feeling really hungry and weak. I looked as white as a ghost. I had a lot of bleeding and cramping. I felt as though I had killed my soul, and knew I had done a terrible thing. I felt so empty. At that moment I lost all respect for myself, or the little I had left. I remember going through the drive-thru of McDonald's on the way home, and ordering a pizza. They had cheap pizzas back then. I looked at my image in the mirror of the car, because I was in the back seat; I was as pale as a sheet of paper.

As soon as I got home, I continued the same old habits. I kept getting into trouble with the law and pretended the abortion was a good decision. Deep inside I had severe depression, anxiety, shame, guilt, and rage all stuffed down inside my heart. I took out these emotions through crime and treating others like dirt, which would momentarily release my pain. I was severely in need of an intervention but there was no one who would give it to me.

It was at this time I had my first taste of crack cocaine, and boy, is that addictive. I remember crawling around the floor looking if I dropped any pieces, so I could smoke more. My boyfriend at the time was needling it and would ask me to pull out the needle from his arms because he couldn't see anymore. I couldn't help him because he had massive hills on his arm and needles grossed me out. I am grateful that I despised needles, because I could have been in for a lot more trouble if I had been hooked on needling my drugs.

It was so insane that there was tin foil on the windows of his home because of the paranoia you have from drugs; you feel you are being watched by cops. I ended up in jail again for charges of theft over $5000, forgery, and arson causing damage to property. By this time I knew what to expect. I was given regular meals and things were safe in jail. I was always put in open custody, which meant I had a lot more freedom than someone who wasn't.

I wasn't placed in a cell, in fact I had my own bedroom. I was placed in a huge home that was for women. I was allowed to go out on passes from time to time. I would go to bars and drink for my allotted time, and then would chew gum prior to signing in for the night. I recall the bed spinning one night when I got back because I had a huge buzz from drinking. I did things I shouldn't have when I was there but my addictions were stronger than me at that time. I believe God was watching over me, though at the time I didn't know it!

When I came out of jail, my household had become worse. My mother hit an all-time low. My step-dad was treating my mum terribly. I tried to get my mum to leave him but she wouldn't. I would throw him out, and she would let him back in. He would keep ringing the doorbell until he got back in. I kept doing drugs and stayed around my mum's more often. I knew she wouldn't leave my step-dad and the only thing I knew to do was to keep my eyes on them. I kept checking in on my mum and brothers more often to make sure they were alright.

My mum kept taking her prescriptions way too fast and would ask us to try to fill them at the pharmacy for her. The pharmacist knew of our situation and would say, "I am sorry but I just filled those yesterday". She learned to doctor hunt and would find someone to fill her prescription so she could get her pills. I knew she was getting worse and it became painful to go there at times.

At this time I had my own apartment and my step-dad wouldn't allow my mother to come over to my apartment alone because he feared I would talk sense into her and get her to leave him. He knew I was a strong person and that scared him. Unfortunately my mother was too sick, and there was no way she was about to change, unless she herself wanted to.

I became pregnant again when I was twenty, and my mum told me to have another abortion. I now know that this is called an atonement pregnancy. I wanted to replace the aborted baby I had lost. I told her I was keeping this baby and was happy. There was no way I could ever have another abortion. The pain of that abortion was unbearable.

I looked at this pregnancy as a second chance to make things right. I was so determined to have this baby that I quit smoking, drinking and doing drugs. I remember lying in my bed and having such withdrawal symptoms, which caused painful headaches.

I was living with the father of my baby and really was determined to give this baby a decent life, a life I only wish I would have had. I wanted to be a mother who was loving, and there emotionally for my child, no matter what. I went over to my mother's house for my usual pop-in visits and she asked me again to fill her pills for her. I said, "No!" and at that moment I heard a voice say to me, "Tell her to write out a will". For some reason I knew deep down inside that my mother was going to die.

My younger brother was on a camping trip at that time with some of my aunts, and my mum was going with my step-dad that weekend to his mother's farm. Part of me wanted to go with her so I asked her, and my step-dad refused to allow me to come along, so I said goodbye to my mum and drove off.

I went about my weekend and on Sunday went for a walk with my boyfriend. That afternoon we walked to my mum's and sat in her backyard and waited for her to get home. After waiting for a while, we decided to leave because she was not coming, which I found a little strange.

We started to walk back to our apartment, and I heard sirens going off and heading out of town. I remember quite distinctly the ambulance sirens and wondering where that accident was that they were going to. Back at my apartment, I went about my day and settled into bed that evening like usual. I was awakened that night, and sat up feeling like something was literally going through my body. I felt like I was on drugs, which was impossible because I had been clean for a few months at this time. I told my boyfriend that something was wrong, that something had happened to someone.

Shortly after this, we heard the knock at the door. Looking out the window, we saw my step-dad leaving our apartment building. I knew at that moment that we had to get dressed and get over to my mum's, quickly. My step-dad would never have come over to my house, not unless something terrible had happened.

The lights were on in my mum's house, but no one was there. I had a really weird feeling as though I were in a fog, feeling like you know something is terribly wrong.

My mum would never leave the doors unlocked and not be home. I went back outside and was going to drive around and look for her until I saw the car lights coming down the street. I waited to see who it was; maybe it was my mum.

It was my step-dad and his mother who pulled up beside me standing there on the front lawn. I looked in the back seat of the car through the window and saw my mum's purse on the seat. "Where is my mum?" My step-dad responded by saying her name and saying, "... is dead". My knees immediately felt like rubber and I fell on the grass outside. My boyfriend, worried about me and the baby, helped me into my mum's house. I remember sitting there in shock despite my premonition. My mother was only forty-three and they had just left to have a nice weekend away. My step-dad's story kept changing as to what happened and clearly at this stage, I thought he had done something to her.

My younger brother was still at the lake with my aunts. Looking back at the situation, I believe that was God's way of protecting my brother from what he might have seen. I knew he had witnessed some horrible stuff like my step-dad hitting my mum in front of him, but to see her die would have been too much. My other brother and I had decided after hearing the news of my mum's death that we should go over to my dad's house. He was after all our father.

My dad answered the door and invited us in. His wife was standing on the staircase and yelled down at us, "Why are you here?" I answered, "Should I go over to the neighbours and ask him to comfort us or should I come here because my dad lives here?" That didn't go over well and my dad pretty much told us to leave and escorted us out. Now I really felt alone and scared.

The next day I went for a walk. I walked past a thrift store we had in town. As I was walking by the store, I noticed some porcelain dolls in the window. They looked like my mum's. I went into the shop and asked the man where he got those dolls. He told me that my step-dad had brought them in that morning.

My mum's house was almost completely cleaned out. As a matter of fact, my step-dad even had a new place rented out within a day of my mother's death. I then had more suspicion in my mind that he had killed her, or had in some way contributed to it.

I had no proof, and the only thing I could think of was to have the police analyse my mother's coffee cup that was in the car the day she died. I thought that possibly my step-dad had put his pills in her coffee to cause her to overdose. Well, that came back negative, and I had nothing to go by.

In hindsight, I know that it is hard to say what happened for sure because my mum had been abusing prescription drugs for years. She also had been hospitalised in the past for taking excess amounts of pills. Even though I felt he had contributed to her death, there was nothing I could do.

At the funeral, my dad and one of my aunts got into an argument in the parking lot over who would get my youngest brother. He was twelve years old, whereas my other brother was eighteen and I was twenty. He ended up having to live with my dad, the dad he never even really knew. My step-mum was quite bitter towards him and eventually social services allowed him to stay with my aunt and uncle who have taken care of him up until this point in time.

I thank God that he got that chance to live with my aunt and uncle, and see what a 'normal' family is like. Being in that situation helped him to avoid making the mistakes I had made. He even finished his schooling.

The following January, I gave birth to a beautiful baby boy. I remember being in labour at the hospital and my boyfriend leaving the hospital to go check on the marijuana plants he was growing. By now I was sober enough for this to really hurt.

Right after I had my son, I felt emotionally depressed and was kept in the hospital for a week because of possible post-partum depression. It was hard not having my mother there to see her first grandchild and to answer the many questions I had about taking care of a baby. On the other hand, it would have been just as difficult to see her so distant from reality and re-live my own experience of her disinterest in babies. I became very over-protective of my son and even had him sleeping in my hospital bed with me. Even when he became older, I would often check to see if he was breathing. I know now that is a symptom from having had an abortion previously. I was afraid he would die. It was a form of anxiety I had to cope with as an aftermath from my abortion.

One evening when my son was a few months old I was sitting in our living room. As I looked over at his toy box, I saw a shadow of a boy about the size my aborted child would have been. That image stuck in my mind, and I wouldn't allow those feelings to surface. I just ignored them and continued to go on with my life. I never wanted to recall that I ever had had an abortion. Slowly, things started to turn bad.

My boyfriend wanted to keep partying and doing drugs and had become physically abusive to me. I guess I stayed with him because I didn't want to be alone, and I felt I didn't deserve any better. I ended up marrying him, even though prior to the wedding I had a feeling in the pit of my stomach that he wasn't the guy for me. He purchased my ring from a pawn shop, which made me feel worthless and ashamed. Before I got pregnant he would sleep around on me and was even intimate with my so-called friends at the time.

Marriage didn't make things better. Drugs, alcohol and partying were things he couldn't part with. He was very emotionally abusive and while I was at work he would do drugs around my son and take him to an out of town bar and drive home after having a few beers.

Finally, even with his father there at the house, my husband choked me. I thought I was going to die. I am grateful his father was there because his father telling him to stop was the only reason he let go. He was then given a restraining order and was no longer allowed to come near me or my home.

The crazy thing is, that day, I went to court and asked the judge to allow him to come home. Fortunately, he made a big scene in the courtroom. He threw a fit and said he didn't want to come home, right in front of the whole courtroom of people. I went home feeling like two cents, knowing that I humiliated myself in letting him come back and even with that I couldn't even get a drug addict abuser to want me. Later that afternoon he called and said he would come home but I had to go sign something at the court house. He did come home and he treated me even worse than he had before.

He cut me down to the point I must have believed what he was saying to have remained in that marriage. Verbal abuse was something I grew up hearing; I didn't deserve any better. Things were so bad that a supervisor where I worked gave me a brochure on divorce and domestic abuse.

Deep inside I could see my past repeating itself in my life and it hurt me deeply to know I had brought a child into this dysfunctional situation even though I knew first-hand the damage it could have on my son. I found out that my husband had slept with someone else. I confronted him on it and he denied it. He kept staying away from home more and would go to his usual bar. I was so hurt that the only thing I knew to do was to get even with him.

I went out one night, had too many drinks and spent the night with a man. The next day, I was so full of shame that I despised myself for what I had done. I felt so low and guilty. My husband found out about this and he was furious. He cheated on me, but when I did the same thing to him, he decided to leave. He packed a suitcase and left.

When he left I was fearful because now I truly was alone to raise our son. I was a co-dependent person and fear consumed me. He kept threatening me even though he had left me. He would plague me with numerous phone calls and tell me he was watching my every move.

I went through a dark phase of heavy drinking and doing drugs, but I believed I had it under control. I was a closet drunk and kept it from my son. I would use alcohol and drugs when he was in bed, or when he was gone with his dad on visits. I became extremely promiscuous and allowed men to use me. I would get drunk and listen to Sarah McLachlan CDs over and over and sing to them with extreme pain in my heart.

I developed obsessive compulsive disorder. I had to check things numerous times like my stove, lights, taps and doorknobs to make sure they were all off. I was never diagnosed with this problem but started taking anti-depressants to cope with my separation anxiety. I took them briefly and threw them out because I didn't want to end up addicted to them like my mother. At least, that is what I thought could happen. I felt so empty inside and had a constant pain in my stomach. I was miserable and in denial. My sins were swallowing me alive. I was in so deep. I was blind to see how my choices were robbing me of peace. Fear consumed my life, or what was left of it.

I quit my job and decided to go back to school and obtain my high school diploma and get a career that could support me and my son. While I was in school, I still had to deal with my son being taken on weekend visits every other weekend, which would be very stressful for him and for me. While on these visits, my son was not taken care of properly. His father was living with his grandmother and he would still continue to go to the bar even though my son was only around him every other weekend. He could not remain sober around his son even though he saw him only periodically.

The cycle of pain was more than obvious when my son started wetting his bed. His father was angry and even told him to key my car when he got home. It killed me to hear some of the things he would do around my son but there was nothing I could do to stop the visits. I could be charged if I tried. I had to live with the fact that my hands were tied.

Hope and Healing… and A New Life Begins

Fortunately, a special woman came into my life. She gave me a Bible and invited me to come to prayer meetings. I was at the bottom of the barrel emotionally at that time and was desperate to find help anyway I could. The thought of having a relationship with God was foreign to me, but I found this woman to be very nice. I started to go to church with my son every once in a while and felt good after I would go.

Somehow I knew that I needed something very different from what I had. In going to church, I had opened a door, but that didn't undo the long progression of events in my life. There were still all kinds of chaos left in my life. These were constant distractions and in a way obstacles that obstructed a clear vision of God, His love and mercy. In the end,

I discovered that while I might have been struggling to see God clearly, He had kept me in His sights and in His love all the way through these trials.

In 2003, I was granted a divorce. The judge gave me a free divorce because he felt this marriage needed to end that very day.

Soon after that, I finished my schooling and was accepted in a course at the Saskatchewan Institute of Applied Science and Technology (SIAST) in Regina. My son and I moved to Regina to an affordable housing complex where we resided for about a year and a half.

During this time, my ex-husband continued to harass me and I just continued to do the best I could to keep my sanity. He would pick up my son from Regina and take him back to his home in Saskatoon. When Sunday would roll around he would call me and tell me his vehicle wouldn't start, and I would have to go get my son. He would tell me that if I didn't come he was going to keep our son and enrol him in school in Saskatoon. He knew he could treat me this way because there was nothing I could do.

In the end, God had the answer. I was overjoyed to find out that my ex-husband moved away and left the province. What a huge blessing for my son and for me. We no longer had to deal with the stress he placed in our lives.

I graduated from my program and decided to move back to my home town where I had a job lined up. Once I got back home I continued to go to church, which was something I had started to do more often. I kept drinking though on weekends, not ready to let that go. It seemed like I was doing everything I could to break the cycle of constant struggle and abuse in my life, but I began to wonder if this was really a possibility when my new boss became difficult, even hitting me in the hands with dental instruments. His treatment didn't go without notice as other staff members told me I should quit. It was easy for them to tell me to do something about it when not one of them would stick up for me when they should have.

I felt ashamed. I had come so far escaping an abusive relationship, a high school dropout who had made it through higher education, raising a son on my own, and here I was again in an abusive situation. How would quitting change anything because I felt like I was destined for this kind of life.

Grace works with nature. Despite my feelings, I had come a long way in changing the path of my life. Even with my failings, I had given God something to work with in my own actions and in my desire to trust Him. I had began to find self-respect.

I finally did walk out when my employer once again disrespected me in front of his patients. I just decided that very second that I would not allow anyone to treat me like that ever again.

I called a lady my aunt knew and asked her to pray with me. I felt kind of silly doing that but I was so desperate that I had to believe there was a God. There had to be more to life than this. I called her up and she prayed for me. She told me that she had a vision of me in the desert like the Israelites and God was leading me out. I did not have a clue as to what she was saying but yet her words comforted me. I then went outside to my vehicle and turned on the ignition. On the radio came words "a change would do you good". The words from that Sheryl Crow song really affected me because I felt like that was God speaking to me through that song. With that leap of faith, I decided to move to Prince Albert and accepted the job I had been offered.

I was always afraid that something would hold me back, something would keep me in the cyclic life of abuse, the only life I knew. It was going to take a great deal of courage to stay the course, not only of trusting God, but of trusting that God had something better in mind for me!

The day I was supposed to move was the weekend before my new job was to start. I remember the night before we had a lot of snow. It was so bad that I was afraid because I had everything packed in the U-Haul for the night and now I was stuck. Well my brothers, my aunt and uncle and I decided to go but we would drive really slowly. We literally had to follow one set of track marks all the way there and hope that no one was coming in front of us. When we got there they helped me and my son get settled into our new apartment and they went home. They were a tremendous help to me and I am grateful for that.

I started my new job and my son started his new school. I had the most wonderful boss who was patient and kind. He treated me with respect, and I believe that I was given that job so I could start to build my relationship with God without added distractions. I needed a safe environment to start to focus on God, not on stress. My son and I attended Mass regularly and he even started to serve at Mass. I started to want to be closer to God but I thought I was the worst sinner ever. I had had an abortion. I had committed adultery and I was divorced. How could God love me? I was ashamed of myself and felt worthless.

I kept living the best I could and eventually was introduced to a special lady and a priest who were to play a special role in my conversion. This woman helped me with all my questions about God and the Catholic faith. We would meet at times and she was always someone I could talk to when I was confused. She blessed me with my first Catholic Bible, a special rosary and numerous other things throughout the years. The priest was from Prince Albert and he was retired, so he had extra time to listen to my long questions.

Soon, I was ready to go to confession. I had not gone to confession since grade two. I had never really known or even thought of going since it was something that was not practiced in my family when I was growing up. It was extremely hard to sit there and tell the priest everything I had done, including my abortion. I thought he was going to look at me like I was disgraceful – but he didn't.

In fact, I felt lighter after I was done. I couldn't believe that I had confided in someone all the pain and sins that I had committed and the priest just listened quietly. He even gave me words of encouragement afterwards and blessed me.

My faith started to blossom to the point that I was going to go to a youth retreat. I had never been to any church activities and this was all new to me. There was confession and music and small group discussions. We were in the church pews and around me were people singing songs that they were familiar with. After a few songs, the presider of the retreat said out loud, "Imagine Jesus is in front of you". Out of nowhere I heard these words, "I am your Father and I love you". I was in so much shock that I looked at my aunt and uncle and told them what had happened; my uncle looked at me kind of funny. I was so excited and all at once had tears of joy. I could not believe that I had heard God speak, let alone to me. These words seemed like they were spoken out but they could have come from within my heart. I was so excited and overwhelmed that I had found out that God is real. He actually exists.

Until that day I had not known what adoration was but now I wanted to be a part of it. I couldn't wait to see what it was. I remember looking around and seeing all these Kleenex boxes on the pews. My thoughts were that adoration must be an emotional time. It was now time for adoration and the priest I knew was saying a lot of blessings. I didn't know what was happening. I remember the tons of thoughts and things I was saying to God in my mind and then I experienced all this love and joy around me. All I could feel was love and joy.

In prayer, I spoke to my grandma on my father's side of the family. I apologised to her for not going to her funeral. I could feel the love. It was so strong that I started to cry.

While this was going on I felt air bubbles rise up from my heart and up through the top of my neck, I was now bawling my eyes out and my shirt was soaked with tears. I believe God had given me a new heart. He had taken my heart of stone and replaced it with a heart of flesh (Ezekiel 36:26).

I was never the same after that adoration and all I could think about was God. After that experience I knew God truly existed. He was real. No one could tell me otherwise. I developed a hunger to read books about God and started learning a whole lot of things I never even knew were possible. Eucharistic miracles, healings, and saints' lives intrigued me. I felt like I had been living in a cave and these things had been kept from me. I couldn't believe that God really exists. He cares for each and every person and He can take time to know our every need, that He understood my pain and was with me the whole time.

God's great mercy is a gift of immeasurable magnitude, but it is not like a fairy godmother who with a swish of a wand makes everything perfect. I had been deeply entrenched in things of the evil one: drugs, sexual immorality, the occult through my mother, and of course the death of my child through abortion.

I was weak and needed to be sheltered from some things at that time. I started to sense things around me at night. I felt as though someone was staring at me and breathing down my neck. I would sleep with the covers over my head.

One night, I remember having been choked in my bed. I would hear noises in my apartment building like doors slamming multiple times. I told the priest about this and he would tell me to call out to Jesus and He would help me. I then started to say 'Jesus' repeatedly until I would fall asleep at night. I even envisioned Mother Mary's mantle wrapped around me as protection.

One day in particular, I was supposed to go back to my home town for a visit. I had my son's bags and my bags packed; I had laid them against the wall in the hallway. I was waiting for the school day to end, and then I was going to pick him up and we would leave from there. I had decided to pray the rosary and as I was praying it, the bags in the hallway started to make a shuffling sound like someone was in them. I got scared and rushed to the phone. I felt at ease for some reason to hope to hear someone's voice. Well, no one answered that call, but I did manage to get my bags out and leave. I went to a payphone and called the priest I knew who came over to bless my apartment.

On Sunday we made our way back home to our apartment. When I opened the door I saw a black mist walk from my kitchen into my living room. I had an eerie feeling. I hadn't seen things since I was a kid and now I was seeing them again. I continued to feel a presence over me at night in my room but I just continued to call out to Jesus. This really showed me that there is a spiritual battle going on for each and every one of us. When I didn't know God it was as though Satan had me, but now that I had turned my life back to God, he was mad. This was how I perceived the situation. I continued to call out to Jesus whenever I felt that presence around me and would ask others for prayer when I felt I needed it.

I finally had a chance to move to a better apartment where I found peace and a quiet absence of all the menacing activity that I had experienced in my old apartment. I will never know if there was terrible activity in that apartment that perpetuated the demonic experience. In my other apartment there were a lot of people whom I could hear fighting regularly. I could smell marijuana in the halls. Once when I was walking towards the laundry room to do my laundry, I had to walk over a man who was passed out in the hallway. Or maybe my own past was haunting me as the devil tried to frighten me into remaining in his clutches. It could have even been my own fears and anxieties had perpetuated the experiences, and I was finally healing enough to find peace. Knowing these things doesn't matter. What matters is that I know that the devil is real and can affect our lives, but that God is king over heaven and earth, over my life and over the demonic forces. As a child of God, I am always under His protection.

I had dear elderly friends who I could attend prayer groups with. I believe God placed elderly women in my life because to me they were like grandma figures. God knows how much my grandma meant to me, and He knows who to place in our paths as we continue to grow. I kept seeking God but still I could feel the shame of my abortion haunting my mind. I would continue to go to confession several times with the sin of my abortion and would just bawl my eyes out in the confessional. Even though the priest told me God had forgiven me I couldn't believe it. I kept getting thoughts that I was going to hell and that I was a murderer. I believed these lies in my head and would push down these emotions as best I could.

I struggled with the desire for my father to love me the way a father should love a daughter, hoping that we would have a relationship now. But his secret visits hidden from his wife made me feel ashamed of myself and angry at him for not being willing to stand up for himself and for his relationship with me.

About this time, I was going to another retreat. My dad had called me out of the blue and had told me that someone had called him about me going to a retreat and that he was asked to write me a letter for encouragement. He basically got mad at me and told me he didn't know what to write. I told him to write whatever he wanted.

At one time during the retreat, the participants were handed out letters from people who knew us. I remember thinking that my letter from my dad would be coming. Well, the first batch of letters that were from our immediate family members came and there was no sign of my letter from my dad. I sunk into a deep despair, feeling like he truly didn't care about me. Soon afterwards we received more letters and there was his letter. I guess there was a mix up with my letters so his came last. I read the letter and was happy to have received one, but I knew that I would have to accept that my father just wasn't capable of the kind of love I needed.

I continued my weekend and couldn't wait to see my son. I had learned a few more things about my faith from that retreat and took from it what I needed at that time. I knew I had a lot of inner healing that needed to be done and I would just continue to turn to Jesus to help me in those areas. I knew I wasn't perfect but with God I felt peace.

Conversion takes time, painfully so. We find ourselves at various stages of conversion until the moment we die. Like a thick onion, I had to allow God to peal back one layer after another. There were so many areas in my childhood where I had not developed and did not understand: trust, genuine love, understanding a father figure, and so many more. God's mercy was always there for me to accept at any moment, but that didn't mean that I automatically understood or trusted. I had to take baby steps, to hold onto something while I walked, then to just stand before I could take my first wobbly steps.

The truth was, I felt lonely. I had been searching my whole life to be special to someone. I knew I was special to God, but the loneliness continued. I visited my brother and his family from time to time and that would make for a temporary respite from the loneliness. But the loneliness would settle back in and I would wonder if that could ever change. I remember the priest I had known had given me some papers to fill out if I ever wished to have an annulment through the Church. I never even knew what an annulment was until this time in my life. I had no clue when I got married how much that decision would affect my life for years to come.

I decided to pursue filling out the paperwork even though I was a single mother who had no intention of ever getting married again. I didn't think anyone would be interested in me or my son and the baggage we came with. I never believed I could find a man who would treat me with love and respect. As a matter of fact, I didn't even know how to allow someone to show me love. I didn't even love myself. I was a damaged woman, who was trying her best to provide for her son. I wanted my son to have a better life than I had had and a mother who loved him no matter what. I loved my son too much to have him grow up like I had. Little did I know that the love I had given to my son and the love that I had received from the elderly ladies at the prayer circles and the patience of the priests and most of all the love of God had been transforming me into someone who could love and be loved.

I liked visiting back home but usually I would feel a lot of emotions come up every time I would go back. All my memories, good and bad, were rooted in that town. I continued to grow in my faith and continued to participate in prayer meetings and attend Mass on Sundays.

I remember one Sunday in particular I was sitting at the back of the church and looking around at all the people in the church. I was wondering if they had problems in their lives like I did. When you have been through so much garbage you tend to feel very alone and that no one understands you. As I was looking around the church, I heard these words, "Not only do you need my love, but all these people need my love". My heart was opening; I was finding healing in seeing the 'other' instead of just seeing myself and my needs.

My loneliness prompted me to start visiting my brother more frequently. One day, I was on his computer looking on the dating site for fun. I noticed a guy on there was from my home town so I showed my brother his picture and he said to me, "Don't laugh Shawna, but I have seen him driving around town, and I think to myself he would be a good guy for you". I thought it strange that my brother would even say something like that to me. Looking back, that must have been the Holy Spirit speaking. My brother knew what kind of car this guy drove and where he worked so I had something to go by. I went back to Prince Albert and during the next week, I thought about this guy, and how I could contact him. In Prince Albert I was friends with and visited a couple from my home town. I went over to their house and told them about this guy and where he worked and what he drove. My friend then said that her friend worked there, so she called up her friend and he happened to know from the description we gave him who he was. I now had a name for this mystery guy. I felt all giddy and like a high school kid. I was scared to call and asked my friend to call him for me. She left a message on his answering machine, and all I could do now was wait.

A week went by and no call back. I then became impatient and decided I had to get the nerve and just call him myself. I called him and he answered. With a leap of faith he was willing to meet a complete stranger at the Boston Pizza restaurant the following Saturday. I was so excited, but nervous, as the week went on. Saturday came and I took my son to my friend's house and I made my way to the restaurant.

This felt like a new chapter of my life. I wanted good things. I wanted a solid role model for my son. I wanted the loneliness in my own life to go away. He was so different than anything I had experienced, having been raised in a secure family without the numerous issues my childhood had brought.

My spiritual journey was two steps forward and one step back. I was still plagued with the many insecurities of being unloved and unlovable. I was still carrying the failures of my past relationships that seemed so good at first and I was inundated with a culture that accepted all kinds of behaviours as not only normal but good. In my brokenness, I rationalised moving in with my fiancé before we were married.

Soon after I moved in, I started to develop anxiety and I actually had an anxiety attack. I was consumed with negative thoughts and decided to try anti-depressants again. A doctor had given me a sample and I felt like I was high. I therefore decided not to go in that direction. Besides, I did not want to be like my mother. For some reason, those pills made me feel shameful and weak. That was not the road I wanted to take. I was seriously being attacked by Satan, because I had opened the door to him once again. The devil loves to take advantage of an open door to harass you, and I had fallen into a trap through my poor decision to cohabitate.

This period of my life was very hard. I had to fight off negative thoughts and wasn't sure what my fiancé was thinking about me. I tried to explain to him about spiritual warfare, and he didn't seem to think that I was crazy. The wedding was getting closer and closer and I had received my notice that my annulment was granted through the mail, which meant I could marry in the Catholic Church. My fiancé was also taking RCIA classes in the Catholic Church to become a Catholic at this time, but we were in too much of a hurry to wait until he was finished the course to get married. The life we were leading meant we couldn't receive Communion on our wedding day.

While so much of this was exciting – discovering I was expecting a child, my wedding and my hope for a new future with my honeymoon – it will also be a memory of a lack of trust in God's ultimate goodness and desire for good things in my life. I know that this was a sin and that sins have concrete consequences in our lives that take time to heal. But I also know that God is merciful and I pray that I will have the strength to be more faithful to His goodness in the future.

Shortly after the honeymoon, I started to have spotting and bleeding. I went to the doctor and was told that can happen. The aunt I had lived with for a short time as a teenager said to me that God was punishing me because I had had an abortion in the past. I couldn't help but wonder if that was true, or maybe for the sin of living together before we were married.

It took me a while to overcome these false thoughts and realise God won't leave me. I may have chosen to separate myself from Him or to not trust Him as completely as I should, but He loves me unconditionally. I also had to realise that while there might be real consequences to sin, even the consequence of not being able to carry a child to full term due to the damage of abortion, this would never mean that God didn't love me.

I remember praying, and crying out to God to please let me keep this baby. I spent many afternoons crying and begging God to hear my prayer. In the meantime, I kept working at the industrial plant and my supervisor would make me do the heavy lifting even though she knew that I was pregnant. The other women who were close friends of hers would laugh and talk about me behind my back. The old lies started working on me. I was back in my home town and the painful memories contributed more to the lie of my not being loved or being capable of giving love. I had abandoned God many times; was God abandoning me?

I was standing in my kitchen in front of the fridge when suddenly a huge gush of blood ran down my legs. I was horrified. We immediately rushed to the hospital. The doctor on call examined me and told me that I was having a miscarriage. He said he had even pulled out a piece of tissue. I was completely heartbroken and saddened. I had planned this baby and desperately wanted to become a mother again. The nurses brought me upstairs to take some pills for pain and to help my uterus contract and expel what was left inside. I said, "No! I am not in any pain, and when I start feeling pain maybe then". When my doctor arrived he sent me to Saskatoon to get an ultrasound to see what was left inside, and to have a D&C (dilation and curettage) if necessary.

While I was getting my ultrasound, the technician said to me, "The heart is strong". I said, "What? You mean the baby is still living?" She replied, "Yes". I explained to her what had happened back home, and how I was glad I hadn't taken those pills.

Could you imagine If I had, I would have had an abortion and not even known. That is scary!

When I came out of the room, I wanted my husband and son to be just as surprised as me, so I waited until we were in the elevator to tell them the news. In the elevator, I pulled out the ultrasound pictures. Both were excited and shocked that I was still pregnant. I was starting to think that God had heard my prayers.

God definitely was protecting my baby. My doctor back home had received the ultrasound results and called me that evening. He was just as confused about the situation as I was. The only thing that sounded plausible was that I could have been carrying twins. Even though I was given the news of possibly being pregnant with twins and could have lost one, I felt relief to know that I was still pregnant.

I was blessed to be able to become a stay-at-home mum, and enjoyed for the first time being home with my son and actually being able to have that option. He, of course, was in school, but he knew now that after school his mum was always home, and I know he appreciated that. With being home and more time on my hands, I started to deepen my relationship with Jesus. I started to pray more often and go to prayer meetings again.

At about 6:00pm, I felt a huge gush of water. My waters had broken! I had never experienced that before either but I knew to go to the hospital right away. We dropped off my son at my aunt's and headed to the hospital. After what seemed hours of pushing, we learned that my baby had the umbilical cord wrapped around his neck and for a few brief moments I was scared until I heard him cry.

My placenta was all torn up and discoloured. In fact, it was sent away for analysis. The doctor had to do a manual scraping of my uterus because my home town didn't have an anaesthetist on call that night either. I was given some kind of freezing and just wanted to see my baby. Shortly after I got home, when I was in bed, I started to sweat terribly and then experienced terrible chills along with cramps and heavy bleeding. I was sent to the city again and had to have a D&C because I had placenta still inside my uterus.

I later learned that because of having had an abortion in the past my uterus could have been scarred. Therefore the placenta had adhered to the uterine wall. Part of my placenta was torn and ripped and some was still stuck inside, which caused me an infection after I had delivered my son. I truly realised how blessed I was to have a healthy baby and to be safe myself.

This time around, I realised I was again becoming an over-protective mum, as I had been with my eldest son. I would check my children at night numerous times to make sure they were breathing. I had fears of them dying, which I believe stems from having had an abortion in my past. I also started to suffer from more aggressive thoughts like, "Why mum? Why am I the one you killed?" Since I was turning to God more now, I also would get thoughts like, "Why even bother? You are going to hell anyway because you killed someone". I remember the weight of this affecting me at times because I wasn't strong enough in my faith to fight off these thoughts. I was still weak and the enemy knew that. The abortion of my past was now starting to haunt me emotionally and spiritually. I would have bouts of crying and wondered if I should listen to these thoughts and just live the way I wanted to.

I remember watching EWTN one day and Mother Angelica was saying that our sins are like a drop of water in the sea of God's mercy. This really made me think and touched me deeply. I wondered if God really could forgive me for the terrible things I had done, especially the abortion.

Soon after that, I was watching a show on Miracle Channel and the host on the show was interviewing a woman who had had an abortion. I couldn't believe that someone was on television admitting she had had an abortion and that she had received healing.

I was just bawling my eyes out in compassion for this woman. I definitely could relate to her. Allowing this to stir up inside of me, I actually felt drawn to share with a woman in my parish about my abortion. I asked her over to my house, and struggled to build up the courage to tell her. I wasn't sure if she would immediately leave or shame me. I took the risk of revealing to her my hidden secret. What she said to me surprised me; a friend of hers was coordinating a Rachel's Vineyard retreat in Saskatchewan. This kind of retreat was new and the first one was to start very soon. I could not believe that there was a retreat that would actually allow post-abortive women to come and seek healing. And it was only twenty minutes from my house.

I was so excited, that I wanted to go immediately. When I look back at this situation, I can again see how God was watching over me, his daughter. I obtained the contact information for the retreat, and I called the lady who was the contact person. I had to wait about a month. I can't remember exactly, but I was counting it down. Finally the day for the retreat arrived!

Warnings of a possible snow storm were announced. I soon began to get the thoughts back. This time they were, "You can't go and leave your husband at home alone with the kids, you will be stuck out there and not be able to get home if there is an accident". I was starting to buy into these thoughts and actually called the contact person to tell her I wasn't sure if I should go because of the storm coming. I only lived twenty minutes away, and she told me there were people who were driving in from British Columbia, and they were fine. It ended up that there was no storm. I felt a little silly and decided to go to the retreat.

After my husband and my sons dropped me off, I immediately felt a terrible loneliness deep inside of me. Soon other women arrived, and the retreat sessions started. I could not believe that there were women all around me who had gone through the ordeal of an abortion. I began to feel safe, and that I wasn't being judged.

Although this was a first retreat, a lot of the women were already working in the pro-life movement. I honestly never really even knew much about pro-life other than the time I had held a sign in Prince Albert, a few years back. I wasn't familiar with any part of it. I remember telling them that I was here for my healing and that, after this, I was not going to be able to tell people I had had an abortion. There was no way I could do pro-life work. I was pretty sure that I was there to receive healing and then put this behind me and move on. During the retreat, I started to question what pain was more painful for me: my childhood or my abortion? I never realised how hurt I really was until the last day of the retreat when I started to cry from the depths of my heart. I couldn't stop crying.

Two women who had come from another province to start the Saskatchewan retreat, took me into a private room. In that encounter, I started to remember the time I came home from school and how my baby brother's hands were burnt from blisters from playing with a lighter when my mum was sleeping. Other painful memories surfaced and within that room, God healed me. I realised I had been robbed of a childhood. It was as though a blindfold was pulled off my eyes and God showed me why I had made the mistakes I made. I was a deeply hurt child.

God sees us from the beginning. He knows each one of us and how our lives were. God doesn't judge the way society judges. God sees all and knows the depths of our hearts. In that room, I had a yearning desire to help troubled kids and was full of joy upon leaving that room.

When it came to sharing my story though, I told the women that during the memorial service for our children, there was no way I could go up and read my letter. They said that was alright.

After lunch, it was time for the memorial service. I had my written note in my pocket, but had no intentions of reading it that day. The time came for us to read our letters, and I heard a voice say to me, "Take out your letter". I took it out of my pocket and looked at it and put it back in my pocket. The voice came again, "Take out your letter". I took it out and felt a hand on my shoulder. I was actually walking up to the podium to read my letter.

I was the first to go up. The lady sitting on the upper balcony doing music ministry said it looked like I was floating up to the podium and walking very gracefully. The Holy Spirit definitely was letting me know that I was to read my letter at that memorial service.

When I left that retreat, I knew I was forgiven by God and by my aborted child (whom I named Michael) and was to let go of all the shame, guilt and unforgiveness I had towards myself. When I got home I would constantly play the music CD

I was given at the retreat. I would sing and cry to God and could feel his presence around me.

From that day forward, I decided to pray the rosary every day, and I promised Mother Mary that was something I would do from now on. I had a hard time praying to Mary before this, partially because of not ever knowing a mother who could really love me and protect me. It took time for that to sink into my mind and heart.

One day I was in the shower praying and I had such a compassion for aborted babies and the women who had had abortions that I would pray and weep for them. This kept happening. I recall going to a local Christian book store and looking at the sales table and seeing the title of a book literally pop out at me - 'Pro-Life Answers to Pro-Choice Arguments'.

I was soon asked to write out my testimony for a lady I had met at the Rachel's Vineyard retreat. I never thought in a million years that I would be writing out my testimony, let alone telling anyone that I had had an abortion. I wanted to take that secret to the grave with me, not reveal it. I prayed about it and asked the Holy Spirit to help me write this testimony if this was what God wanted. I had a pen and paper beside me; my pen literally flew for 45 minutes. I had a testimony, but now what?

God guided me through my journey, and I was asked to go to the Millennium Cross for the unborn, in Aberdeen. I would share my story. The Millennium Cross is a huge cross placed in the field off the highway and every year people gather to pray for the unborn and for an end to abortion. The night prior to this, I attended adoration and asked God that if this be His will for me, He would show me during adoration.

On the drive home, I listened to the CD I had been given at the Rachel's Vineyard retreat. I was listening to the song 'A Baby's Prayer'. I started to feel strength and compassion within my heart bubble up. I was in tears, and knew I had to do this, no matter how hard it was. Late that night, I began to hear scratching noises, and I asked my husband, "Are you hearing this?" We both heard the noises and checked around for the cause. Nothing was out of sorts in the house as far as we could see. The noises continued, and I said out loud, "I know where this is coming from. I am still going to share my story tomorrow". The noises stopped, but I started to shake and was literally freezing; my teeth were chattering. I didn't sleep much that night, and I remember the next morning feeling like a zombie because I was so tired.

I went to the Millennium Cross site and, as scared as I was, heart racing, full of fear, I told my story for the first time. It felt good to be able to do that. I couldn't believe I had managed to do it. I was starting to see God at work in my life and how He was with me the whole time. I could never have done this if it wasn't for God. He is amazing.

I was growing in a relationship with God, and continued to go to retreats and prayer meetings.

I was meeting great people who would pray with me and showed me they truly cared for me. It started with grandma figures. God would place elderly women in my life to plant seeds in my heart. Looking back now I see why God did that. My own grandma meant so much to me, and God was giving me that gift. The only person I would have listened to would have been my grandma.

I had to come to the conclusion that life is a journey of conversion and forgiveness.

There are many trials in life, and having come from such a dysfunctional past, I needed an extra push along the way. I had tried throughout the years to have a relationship with my dad but he wants nothing to do with me or my brothers. I had to go back to those words God spoke to me at a retreat, "I am your Father, and I love you".

I have had to go back to those words many a time to let go of the pain of rejection that my father had caused me. I realise now that God is truly my Father. That is why He gave me those words. It is absolutely incredible to see how God can work in our lives if we let Him enter our hearts.

If it weren't for God, who knows where I would be today. I am grateful to God for my second chance to live a life that pleases Him. My life isn't perfect, but knowing God now and placing him in the centre of my life is what gets me through the storms ahead.

I went through a crisis in my marriage, and I was glad to have God with me through this hard time. I have seen how God healed my husband and restored our family. Without prayer I can't imagine what would have happened to my family. God loves us so much and is waiting at the door of our hearts. He wants a personal relationship with each one of His people. I thank God every day for my life and what He has done through and with me. He simply amazes me, and I am excited to walk with Him and to see where He leads me.

I can now look back at my past and be grateful for it. I would never have come to know God, if I hadn't gone through these trials. I had to find myself at the bottom of the barrel in my own life to come to recognise that God is real. He was right there waiting that whole time for me to come back to Him. It brings me to tears to think of how painful it was for Him to watch me, His daughter, fall into such bad choices. My life is now dramatically changed because He is such a loving Father, because of the love He has for me. Things aren't always perfect, but now I turn to God in prayer and I realise He is there and knows what is best for me. He continues to heal me each day and I know to thank Him along the way as I journey through life.

Reflections and Prayers

Stepping out in faith

Since the day God touched my heart in a profound way, I can say I am certain that He is with me. I know He is around me every step I take and every time I fall, He is there to pick me up. There are going to be days when we can't understand why God allowed certain things to take place in our lives. Believe me when I say, that faith can pull you through those tough times. Have faith that God knows what is best even though we cannot see the whole picture all the time. God can turn a mess into a message, and when we step out in our lives He is with us every step of the way.

Pray for their souls

"Do not be overcome by evil, but overcome evil with good,"
(Romans 12:21).

A few days ago I was overcome with anger and frustration of things going on around me. This led me to use my anger in a sinful manner. My emotions got the best of me that day. I turned to God and asked for His forgiveness. I asked Him to help me to improve my character when anger seems to get the best of me.

Yesterday while I was driving a man cut me off when I had the right of way. He then proceeded to give me a gesture which would have normally caused anger to arise in me. By God's grace I then prayed for this man's soul and that he would come to know God and be able to release his anger to God, and for him to be healed. Then as I proceeded down the highway home, a truck passed me and a rock hit my newly-replaced car windshield. The grace God gave me kept me from using anger in an ungodly way.

Dear Lord,

Thank you for the graces you give us. Thank you for helping me to grow and learn from my mistakes. I am sorry when I do things that lead me to sin, and I need you to help me back up when I fall. Help us all Lord to be able to do our best and learn from our mistakes. Amen.

Bless them

"Bless those who persecute you; bless and do not curse them," (Romans 12:14).

This Scripture can be very challenging for us if we can't see with eyes of compassion. Hurting people hurt others is a saying I believe and know from my own past experiences. The real challenge is rising above our own fleshly emotions and praying for those who hurt us, instead of lashing out at them.

Dear Jesus,

Help us to see with eyes of compassion. Help us to recognise that we need to pray for others who are hurting. Help us to be more like you. With your grace I know we can bless our fellow neighbours. Amen.

Division in family

"Do you think that I have come to give peace on earth? No, I tell you, but rather division; for henceforth in one house there will be five divided, three against two and two against three; they will be divided, father against son and son against father, mother against daughter and daughter against her mother, mother-in-law against her daughter-in-law and daughter-in-law against her mother-in-law," (Luke 12:51-53).

This was the Scripture passage my priest gave a homily on at Mass recently. I have had relationships in my life that I have had to walk away from because of the pain they caused me. I have changed for the better because Christ lives in me. I am a new creation and the old me has died because of Christ. There are family members in my life who find it hard to be around me now because I have changed so much. I am no fun to them anymore. Personally, I don't live for the world anymore, I live for God. It is very painful to be separated from them, and I pray for their conversions every day.

Dear Lord,

You know the pain this causes us to have to let go of the people we love. I pray that they will see the truth someday, in your time Lord. That they will realise that you are real and that you love them very much. I pray for their conversion, and that their hard hearts will melt as you hold them in your hands. Give us the strength to persevere in prayer for our loved ones as we wait for their conversions. Amen.

Love them

"But I say to you that hear, love your enemies, do good to those who hate you, bless those who curse you, pray for those who abuse you," (Luke 6:27-28).

It took me a long time to get to the point where I can now honestly say, I obey this passage in my own life. It speaks volumes of truth, and WILL lead you to a peaceful life. At times it was so hard to overcome this; my flesh fought my spirit tooth and nail. That doesn't mean I don't struggle at times in this area. I realise that I need to pray for humility everyday to overcome my flesh. I have seen the peaceful reward that accompanies being faithful to His word.

Dear Jesus,

Thank you for guiding us and loving us. Lord help us to be more like you. Cleanse us and purify our hearts. I pray for those who have come from a past like mine who struggle in this area. I pray for humility, and healing of their hearts. Lord, thank you for your patience as we grow to know you more and more each day. Amen.

Have you truly let go?

I sensed a changed in my heart and with that I was tested. These last few weeks I have had to truly search inside my heart and release all to God. I had to 'let go' and surrender all of myself into His hands and TRUST in Him to bring the pieces together according to His plan. That meant allowing Him to take all that I was clinging to, and to give it to Him even though fear gripped me.

Dear God,

I am sorry for my lack of trust in you at times. Please forgive me. I am weak and I need you to give me strength. Thank you Father for this test of faith that has brought me closer to knowing your love for me. I pray for all people to come to know you at a deeper level, and to truly allow you to direct their lives. Amen.

Can you turn your cheek?

"You have heard that it was said, 'An eye for an eye and a tooth for a tooth'. But I say to you, do not resist one who is evil. But if anyone strikes you on the right cheek, turn to him the other also," (Matthew 5:38-39).

Have you been hurt so badly by someone that your flesh bubbles up in anger? Do you feel like exposing their falsehoods? Is that the way God would want us to handle the situation?

I know and believe that the most honourable thing to do in any situation like this is to place it in God's hands. It shows more courage and strength to 'give it to God' than to allow your flesh to have its way. This is the true test of God; can you walk the walk instead of talking the talk, so to speak. The path that leads to Christ is a very narrow path. It takes strength, trust, and perseverance, and the peace that comes after each test is very rewarding.

Dear Jesus,

I pray for each and every person who is tested in this area. I know there are times we will fall, and I know, Jesus, you will be there to pick us up each and every time. I pray for strength, healing and trust for those enduring this test in their lives. We need to love others, and forgive each other, over and over again. Amen.

Confidence in God

"Hence we can confidently say, 'The Lord is my helper, I will not be afraid; what can man do to me?'" (Hebrews 13:6).

Have you been hurt, rejected, and ridiculed? I am sure we all have been at one time or another. Yes it hurts; yes it can wound us deeply. We can either allow that pain to fester in us and eat us alive, or we can give it to God. God is your helper, He loves you. Make your heart right with Him. Don't be afraid.

Dear Lord,

I pray for those of us who have been wounded, rejected, and hurt deeply by others. You love us all so much. I pray that you will change our hearts and theirs. That you would be the centre of our lives. Lord, give us the confidence to stand tall knowing that you are with us each step in our day. Amen.

Helping the lost

"Let him know that whoever brings back a sinner from the error of his way will save his soul from death and will cover a multitude of sins," (James 5:20).

Having been saved from my sinful past, I can see now how my sins almost gripped the life out of me. There are people who come into my life and I find they are caught up in things that used to consume me before I knew God. Things of this world and addictions that once had a hold of me.

I know now that I am to be an example of God's grace. A light in this dark world. Although I feel their pain and hope they could stop what they are doing instantly, all I can do is be an example. Your life can be instrumental in one's conversion if you allow God to work through you to help the lost.

Dear Lord,

I thank you for the lost people you have placed in my life. I ask that you would help me to keep being a light for those in need. Please give me the right words and open their hearts to you, Father. Amen.

His power is made perfect in weakness

"But he said to me, 'My grace is sufficient for you, for my power is made perfect in weakness'. I will all the more gladly boast of my weaknesses, that the power of Christ may rest upon me. For the sake of Christ, then, I am content with weaknesses, insults, hardships, persecutions, and calamities; for when I am weak, then I am strong," (2 Corinthians 12:9-10).

I have been really tested these last few weeks. I have had to swallow my own pride and allow humility to shine through me. This has been a real awakening of virtues and lessons in my life. God has been shaping me and moulding me and although I have shed many tears I know He is doing this all for my good. He loves me so much that He is taking my weaknesses and guiding me to use them as strengths.

Dear Jesus,

I love you so very much. I know that you are with me always. You hear my cries, and see my growth. I thank you for these lessons. I ask that you give me the strength to rise above and grow to become a better person. Amen.

Rescue me Lord

"Be gracious to me, O God, for men trample upon me; my enemies trample upon me; all day long foemen oppress me; my enemies trample upon me all day long, for many fight against me proudly. When I am afraid, I put my trust in thee. In God, whose word I praise, in God I trust without a fear. What can flesh do to me? All day long they seek to injure my cause; all their thoughts are against me for evil. They band themselves together, they lurk, they watch my steps," (Psalm 56:1-6).

Fear has been consuming me these last few months. I have been struggling with making a decision based on the hold fear had over me. I was just reminded by a wise priest that life is full of risks. Trust God, and have faith. With that being said, I let go of the fear that was paralysing me, and made a decision in faith. I could feel an instant weight being released from me after I let go and trusted God.

Dear Lord,

I pray for all those people who are bound up in fear. I pray for strength and courage for them. Jesus, you know what is best for us and we trust in you. Amen.

Seek peace

"For he that would love life and see good days, let him keep his tongue from evil and his lips from speaking guile; let him turn away from evil and do right; let him seek peace and pursue it," (1 Peter 3:10-11).

Have you ever been frustrated with someone? Have you ever been picked on and treated poorly? At these moments have you felt anger boil up and have you caught yourself falling into sin with your tongue?

We all have, we all fall short. The moment after we have sinned this way we feel worse than before. What is the answer to this? I do know the times I have held back my tongue I have recognised God's grace in my life. When I feel weak in these moments I ask God for His help and His strength to rise above this temptation of sin. We are called to be imitators of Christ, are we not? In these situations when I have done the right thing there always is a peace that follows. The more we work on being imitators I know God will bless us.

Dear Father,

I pray that you would give each of us the strength to rise above our temptations. Please give us the grace to be imitators of you. Help us to love each other and to build each other up, instead of tearing each other down. Amen.

He is waiting

"Draw near to God and he will draw near to you," (James 4:8).

The first part of this Scripture shows us how much God truly loves us. The minute we call out to Him, He is at our side. Eagerly waiting for us to call unto Him, patiently He waits. Time and time again He shows me how much He loves me.

Everyday I pray and ask God to help me get through my day, and with that my day has meaning. I see things in a whole new way even when the day doesn't go the way I hoped it would; I have faith that God is with me. Knowing He is with me gives me strength to try to be a good example even when times are tough. We all slip and fall, but let's ask God to be near us to pick us up again.

Dear Jesus,

I thank you for today and all that you do in our lives. I pray that all people would recognise how much you love them. You patiently wait at the door and knock, hoping they answer. I pray they answer and draw close to you, where they will be loved. Amen.

My family

"Above all hold unfailing your love for one another, since love covers a multitude of sins," (1 Peter 4:8).

We are all sinners, nobody is perfect. We have good times, and we have not so good times. The key to a strong family foundation is to 'love' each other through these times. Talking things out and supporting each other in our weaknesses helps us to grow in love and understanding for each other.

Dear Jesus,

I pray for all families. I pray especially for those who are struggling within their own family relationships. I ask that they are given strength and grace to work through their problems and to keep you at the centre of their lives. Without you Jesus, there is no hope. Amen.

Keep your eyes on Jesus

"We are afflicted in every way, but not crushed; perplexed, but not driven to despair; persecuted, but not forsaken; struck down, but not destroyed; always carrying in the body the death of Jesus, so that the life of Jesus may also be manifested in our bodies. For while we live we are always being given up to death for Jesus' sake, so that the life of Jesus may be manifested in our mortal flesh," (2 Corinthians 4:8-11).

Life is hard, trials can be burdensome. We can crash and hit the ground. When we are hurt it is easy to focus on our own pain and have the 'poor me' or 'what about me' attitude. But is that right? Is this not sin to reflect on ourselves; could it be idolatry?

We need to turn that around and focus on Jesus, not ourselves. If we are being hurt over and over again we need to pray for the person who is hurting us. No one said it would be easy, but with God all things are possible. If you have allowed anger, stress, and frustration to knock you down, do the opposite and get back up. Ask for God's grace and start anew. Keep your eyes on the prize that awaits you in heaven.

Dear Jesus,

Please forgive us for focusing on ourselves and not on you. Jesus you are all loving, and forgiving. Give us the strength to do what is right. Help us to be better examples of you and to know that we can do all things because you dwell in our hearts. You are our strength and we need you. Amen.

A gentle reminder

"And let us not grow weary in well-doing, for in due season we shall reap, if we do not lose heart," (Galatians 6:9).

I was having a challenging week and was feeling frustrated and down. When Saturday came along I went shopping for a few items. In line at Costco a kind stranger started making chit-chat with me and told me I could go ahead of her. Having thanked her, I startled her with how much I appreciated her kindness. Then I headed to Sears to find a longer winter coat. To my surprise they were 50 percent off that day. I went to the ladies' coat section and started looking through the racks at what was left. Once again a kind stranger gave me the coat she had in her hand and told me to try it on. She told me it did not fit her and it was the only one left in that size. I tried on the coat, and it was exactly what I was looking for. It fit me like a glove. I thanked her and told her how it had been a blessed day, and how much I appreciated this.

This incident reminded me that God works through others. These strangers had made my day with their actions. God showers us with love and blessings if we take the time to appreciate and see the good in even the small and simple things in our day. Just think if we could all try to show kindness, how we could make even one person have a day that reflects God's love for them.

Dear Jesus,

I pray that we can all grow in love for one another. That we could slow down from this busy world and take the time to be a blessing to someone. Amen.

Give it all to God

"Have no anxiety about anything, but in everything by prayer and supplication with thanksgiving let your requests be made known to God. And the peace of God, which passes all understanding, will keep your hearts and your minds in Christ Jesus," (Philippians 4:6-7).

We all have stress in our lives. I am sure we have all had anxiety, or still can suffer from anxiety from time to time. When we realise that we are stressed and feel burdened it is hard to automatically just give it to God at times. We like to carry our burdens, and sometimes even sit in our misery before we can let go. I know from personal experience that when I hand it over to God right away, I do feel a lot better than when I sit in my own misery. There is definitely a peace that follows that right decision to let go and let God carry my burden. Letting go is a very hard thing to do but with the help of the Holy Spirit we can let go and find freedom.

Dear Jesus,

I pray for all of us who struggle with anxiety. That you could give us the strength to keep trusting in you, and handing over our struggles to you each day. That we could feel a deep peace when we surrender our hurts and struggles into your hands. Jesus, we trust in you. Amen.

Give us the grace, O Lord

"Have I not commanded you? Be strong and of good courage; be not frightened, neither be dismayed; for the Lord your God is with you wherever you go," (Joshua 1:9).

The words spoken above tell us that God is with us all the time and not to fear. So why do we struggle with this? Why does fear come over us at times? Personally, I have struggled with anxiety all my life. My past was full of chaos, stress, and hardships. I have had to deal with fear and anxiety a large percentage of my life. Even though I know God is real and that God is truly in my life, I still can fall into anxiety. This is who I am. I have learned to pray and ask God to help me. I know that even though I am like this, God still loves me. He will not leave me. He will not abandon me.

Dear Jesus,

I pray for all those who struggle with anxiety and fear. I pray for those children who are in dysfunctional homes who are hurting and need someone to love them. I ask that they would come to know you in their lives and that with your help you can help them to live the life you have for them. Amen.

Your faith has made you well

"And he said to her, 'Daughter, your faith has made you well; go in peace, and be healed of your disease'," (Mark 5:34).

It has been 20 years since I chose to have an abortion. My life was a cyclone of addiction, abuse, and a heart that was terribly broken from my dysfunctional life. I was a hurting girl who needed guidance and love. I was lost and felt alone. The thought of even knowing God seemed weird and foreign to me. I thought this was the life I was destined to live feeling trapped in dysfunction and pain.

Looking back today I cannot believe that was me. I was so lost and had a hardened heart full of pain. I was at the point of death and then I met Jesus. Having allowed Jesus into my life was when the transformation started to happen over time. He worked on me slowly and allowed me to trust Him completely so He could complete a work in my life. I surrendered to Him and allowed Him to cleanse my heart and restore me to be the woman He created me to be.

Dear Jesus,

I thank you for loving me and for healing my heart. I pray for all people who are suffering, that they would turn to you for healing and comfort. Without you we cannot be healed; we need you. Amen.

Believe that God will protect him

"Train up a child in the way he should go, and when he is old he will not depart from it," (Proverbs 22:6).

This week my eldest son graduates from high school, and it is a new phase for me in my life as well. He is off to university this fall many miles away from us. That was hard to hear at first when he decided to choose a place so far away. I got adjusted to this choice after some time and was excited he was going to pursue an education. Just a few weeks ago he told us he is going to Brazil for three weeks over the summer to meet his girlfriend of two years now.

My first reaction was anger followed by more anger. My son has never flown on a plane, let alone gone all alone to Brazil. He had told me he had planned everything and was quite confident he would be safe and knows what he is doing. I learned through this that I once again have to let go and trust God and believe that my son will make positive choices. We raised him with good morals and I pray for my boys everyday. In the past couple of weeks I have allowed God to be in control of this decision; my worrying will not change the circumstances or the outcome. I had to believe in the verse I had written above from Proverbs, which kept echoing in my mind as I wrote this reflection.

Dear God,

Please watch over our children as they grow up and become adults. Even though they don't need us to physically take care of them we still grieve that little child we took care of. I pray as they make choices in life that they will remember their faith and continue to seek you in their lives. Amen.

In the midst of a storm

"Blessed is the man who endures trial, for when he has stood the test he will receive the crown of life which God has promised to those who love him," (James 1:12).

The last week has been really trying for me. I have been through some pretty stressful situations. I was doing well until the last trial; it broke me emotionally. As tears streamed down my face I wondered why? Why do I have to keep getting hurt over and over again? I was questioning God as I poured my heart out in tears. I soon realised that I was falling into self-pity and then apologised to God. Having asked someone to pray for me and turning to God was the start of letting go of something I could not control. As much as the situation killed me inside I had to realise that ONLY God can change this outcome. In less than a day the situation was resolved and peace started to take over. Even in my weakness He still shows me He loves me and blesses me.

Dear Jesus,

Thank you so much for being at my side through this trial. It is hard at times when we keep getting hurt again and again to not fall into sin. With your strength all things are possible and I thank you for strengthening me in these times of trial. I pray for all the people who are hurting to keep giving you their hurts so they can be healed and grow in their faith. Amen.

Change is possible with Christ

"And he fell to the ground and heard a voice saying to him, 'Saul, Saul, why do you persecute me?' And he said, 'Who are you, Lord?' and he said, 'I am Jesus, whom you are persecuting; but rise and enter the city, and you will be told what you are to do'," (Acts 9:4-6).

Have you been hurt by others? Have you been judged, talked about falsely? Treated unfairly? We all can say 'yes' I am sure. The question is how did you respond? Did you recognise that you are hurting God when we treat others poorly? We are called to be 'one body in Christ', loving each other even in times when it is hard. This is possible by recognising that this person who is hurting you is obviously hurting deeply themselves. They are in need of prayer. If anger arises from us being treated harshly, take that to the confessional. We need God's grace to be loving, and only He can transform our hearts. I know the power of change, and God can transform us like He did St Paul. Pray for the people who hurt you and I promise in God's timing you will see real change.

Dear Jesus,

Give us the grace to rise above our anger when we are treated poorly. Help us to forgive, and pray for those who hurt us. Transform their hearts to see that with your help their lives could be transformed. Amen.

Restore me Lord

"Create in me a clean heart, O God, and put a new and right spirit within me. Cast me not away from thy presence, and take not thy Holy Spirit from me. Restore to me the joy of thy salvation, and uphold me with a willing spirit," (Psalm 51:10-12).

Have you searched down deep in your heart? Have you seen the things hidden down deep? We all need cleansing in our hearts. We need to allow the Holy Spirit to speak to our hearts and help us to acknowledge our sins. Once we 'let go' of the garbage we are hanging on to, and allow God to work in our hearts, we will then find true joy. This is something we need to keep seeking daily as we grow in faith and trust. With the help of the Holy Spirit let us seek joy and peace and not allow the stress we face to make a home in our hearts.

Dear Jesus,

Thank you for loving us. I pray for all people who are facing struggles and stress in their lives. For the ones who so desperately seek joy and peace. Please cleanse and purify our hearts and give us the grace to let go of the stress we are carrying. Amen.

Love

"Love is patient and kind; love is not jealous or boastful; it is not arrogant or rude. Love does not insist on its own way; it is not irritable or resentful; it does not rejoice at wrong, but rejoices in the right. Love bears all things, believes all things, hopes all things, endures all things," (1 Corinthians 13:4-7).

This Scripture reminds us how to show true love from the heart. Love that is pure, not tainted from our own dysfunction. We need to be reminded to show love, even when we are hurt by someone and we are angry at them. Time and time again I have been tested in this area. I have failed in the past, but I am getting better at loving now. The way I overcome my weakness in this area is to remember that when someone hurts me or treats me poorly, it is because they are hurt themselves. Hurt people hurt others. We need to look at others with eyes of compassion and with empathy and then we can start to bear fruit in this area, and grow in love.

Dear Jesus,

I am sorry when I have failed to grow in love for others. When I have been selfish and allowed my own feelings to harden my heart towards others who have hurt me. Please help me to grow in love for others and to forgive those who have hurt me. Amen.

Have faith in God

"When the righteous cry for help, the Lord hears, and delivers them out of all their troubles. The Lord is near to the broken hearted, and saves the crushed in spirit," (Psalm 34:17-18).

A few weeks back I was given some surprising news from someone close to me. This person was choosing to go down a road that I was shocked to see them take. Although I knew they were making a terrible choice that pained me, it was something I had to let go of. I had mentioned my concerns with them and how much I cared for their wellbeing. At first anxiety grew inside me as I wrestled with the fact I was not in control, but as my heart grew anxious I had to place my faith in God and trust Him. I released my anxiety, anger, and broken heart entirely into God's hands. Within a few weeks I noticed a change in how I felt about the situation. Sure, I was still concerned for that person but I truly felt that God lifted the burden from me. Inside I feel a deep peace and a sense of wisdom about the situation. I know only God could have calmed my anxious heart.

Dear Jesus,

Thank you so much for loving us. I know you are in control of our lives and I am sorry when we try to control them ourselves. You know what is best for us and I know you are always near. Help our faith to increase. Amen.

He will lead you

"It is the Lord who goes before you; he will be with you, he will not fail you or forsake you; do not fear or be dismayed," (Deuteronomy 31:8).

Do you believe God is with you at all times? Do you trust Him? I know that if God is leading you into something He most definitely will protect you and He is always faithful. That does not mean that fear won't try to engulf you at times, but with each act of courage and faith you will see how His promise is true. When you truly believe and trust in God your fears dissolve. In the past I would fail at trusting and would be anxious and doubtful. It took me awhile to build up my faith and trust in God's love for me. I failed many times until I trusted fully and let go of my own insecurities and weaknesses. Next time you feel called to do something for God, just take a step in faith and see what happens, if you struggle at first just try again.

Dear Jesus,

Thank you for loving us and watching over us at all times. I pray for strength and perseverance in faith to let go and trust in you. To be able to release our anxiety and fear and replace it with peace and trust. Amen.

Who are you to judge?

"The scribes and the Pharisees brought a woman who had been caught in adultery and placing her in the midst they said to him, 'Teacher, this woman has been caught in the act of adultery. Now in the law Moses commanded us to stone such. What do you say about her?' This they said to test him, that they might have some charge to bring against him. Jesus bent down and wrote with his finger on the ground. And as they continued to ask him, he stood up and said to them, 'Let him who is without sin among you be the first to throw a stone at her'. And once more he bent down and wrote with his finger on the ground. But when they heard it, they went away, one by one, beginning with the eldest, and Jesus was left alone with the woman standing before him. Jesus looked up and said to her, 'Woman, where are they? Has no one condemned you?' She said 'No one, Lord'. And Jesus said, 'Neither do I condemn you; go, and do not sin again'," (John 8:3-11).

Are we not all sinners? We all fall short when it comes to sin. No one is perfect. We all fall and get back up with God's grace. People can make poor choices due to their own brokenness. Jesus can see our hearts and why one might have gone down the wrong road and what led them to poor judgment.

The reason I wrote this book was to show people that no matter how lost you are, or rejected you feel, God is there waiting to restore you.

He knows your heart and what led you to those crippled choices.

I also remember years ago being at prayer meetings and hearing 'believers' judge others for sins they heard they committed. I recall sitting there and shaking, wanting to stand up and say, 'Who are you to judge, you do not know that person, or what led them to that choice?' The reason I did not say anything at the time was because I was weak and felt afraid to say anything.

Sin is horrible and has terrible consequences, I get that. I also know what it feels like to be that hurting person trapped in sin. Instead of judging other people we need to be more compassionate and reach out our hand to the one who is drowning in pain. Our compassion and love will lead that person to Christ, I promise you it will. We are more likely to reach people in love than in hate.

Dear Jesus,

I thank you for loving us. I thank you for restoring my broken heart. I pray for all who are hurting and suffering, that you will heal their hearts. I pray for others to look with compassionate eyes and be the light that will draw others out of darkness. Amen.

Are you wearing a mask?

"Take no part in the unfruitful works of darkness, but instead expose them," (Ephesians 5:11).

Are you wearing a false mask? Are you pretending to be perfect? Do you realise the spiritual effects this false appearance can have on you?

In order to start the process of healing you need to be honest with yourself and Jesus. Bringing the things you have hidden in the dark to Jesus will produce a light that will shine and bring you closer to Him. In time He will free you and give you a peace that only comes from knowing Him. You need to be real with yourself if you desire change. If you are tired of going in circles and not being at peace, Jesus is only a prayer away.

Dear Jesus,

I pray for all people who are suffering and distressed. People who are afraid to admit they are hurting. I pray they will come to know you and seek the peace that only you can give them. Amen.

A mother's heart

"Train up a child in the way he should go, and when he is old he will not depart from it," (Proverbs 22:6).

Today I was looking through some Christmas ornaments and I came across this special one my eldest son had given me a long time ago. After reading the message on the ornament I began to tear up; I have not seen my son in nine months and miss him dearly. This Scripture in proverbs reminded me that God gifted us with him, and as parents our job is to raise our children to become independent, responsible individuals. As hard as it is to see them move away and grow up, I can say I accomplished my task. I pray daily for my children and know that Jesus is with them watching over them daily.

Dear Jesus,

I thank you for watching over our children as we place them in your hands every day. I pray for those who miss their children and cannot see them that often, that you will fill the hole they have in their hearts with peace. Amen.

He is hope

"For to us a child is born, to us a son is given; and the government will be upon his shoulder, and his name will be called Wonderful Counsellor, Mighty God, Everlasting Father, Prince of Peace," (Isaiah 9:6).

Hope is the word that comes to my mind when I ponder Christ's birth. He is the answer to restoring our brokenness and filling us with the peace that only comes from knowing Him. I have to honestly say that Christmas was a holiday that left me feeling sad, empty, and depressed in the past. Having not had a family home or parents of my own to be with, it caused deep sadness within me. Now I can say that Christmas gives me hope. Hope that has restored my broken heart and given me a deep love for the Prince of Peace, my Everlasting Father.

Dear Jesus,

I thank you for all you have done in my life. I pray for those who suffer with sadness and emptiness over the holidays. May they find the true meaning of Christmas and turn to you to fill them with hope and love. Amen.

A new life, a fresh start

"And you, who once were estranged and hostile in mind, doing evil deeds, he has now reconciled in his body of flesh by his death, in order to present you holy and blameless and irreproachable before him, provided that you continue in the faith, stable and steadfast, not shifting from the hope of the gospel which you heard, which has been preached to every creature under heaven, and of which I Paul, became a minister," (Colossians 1:21-23).

I personally enjoy reading the writings from Paul the apostle. The deep love he has for God and his gift of faith can minister to our hearts. I can relate to this passage very much in the sense of how Jesus can transform our lives if we trust and keep persevering. Jesus can restore your life, and make you holy. My past was not a very easy one, I was doing evil deeds and far from God. If you asked me twenty years ago if I thought I could have a good, healthy life I most likely would have doubted that. Where I was then and where I am now is like night and day. Start seeking Jesus and ask Him into your heart, and in time your faith will grow and your hope will increase. The only way to move past the evil and brokenness in our lives is through knowing Jesus.

Dear Jesus,
I pray for all those who are hurting and suffering. People who are trapped in darkness and are unaware of your love for them. I pray for them to come to know of your goodness and love. Amen.

Call upon Him

"For, 'Everyone who calls on the name of the Lord shall be saved'," (Romans 10:13).

Do you believe this? Do you believe that Jesus loves you enough to save you, by just crying out to Him?

I hope you realise the answer is 'yes', He loves you unconditionally and is waiting with open arms for you to return to Him. No matter how far you strayed from Him, know that He was and is always with you. I share this passage with real truth on this matter, I had once strayed from Jesus. I made poor choices that led me on a road of shame, guilt, anger and deep sin. I was hurting so badly, I grasped worldly fixes that spiralled down a web of sin. One poor choice led to another, and to another. When I had hit rock bottom in my despair I cried out to Jesus and that was the start of my healing journey. I took the first step by calling on His name and He met me where I was at in my life. With little steps in the right direction I soon began to notice Jesus was healing my brokenness.

Dear Jesus,

I thank you for what you have done and are doing in my life right now. I pray for the people who are lost in despair and sin. I pray they will cry out to you and see the love you have for them in your heart. Amen.

What is hidden in your heart?

"Praise the Lord! For it is good to sing praises to our God; for he is gracious, and a song of praise is seemly. The Lord builds up Jerusalem; he gathers the outcasts of Israel. He heals the broken hearted, and binds up their wounds. He determines the number of the stars, he gives to all of them their names. Great is our Lord, and abundant in power; his understanding is beyond measure," (Psalm 147:1-5).

Have you ever felt like you were past something, that you had already dealt with it and did not realise you still had hidden anger? That what you thought you moved on and made peace with still left a scar in your heart? That you indeed have hidden pain that ran deeper than you thought?

I lost my mother tragically when I was twenty years old. It was unexpected and shook me to the core. Although there were circumstances that I knew would eventually lead to her premature death, it still was shocking for me. I thought I was past the anger and sadness of her life cut short… but clearly it was still there buried in my heart.

I recently lost my father-in-law to a battle with cancer. He was the dad I never had. I have not lost anyone this close to me since my mum's passing and it opened the door to anger I thought I had dealt with. Hidden anger I had from the past; the pain of losing my own mother too soon. Grief can bring out many emotions within us, good and bad and we need to recognise it and voice it to those who support us. When emotions come up we need to ask God to heal our brokenness and to restore our lives. He is an understanding Father and can see deep into our hearts the pain we are burying. The anger will become less if we can recognise it and trust in Jesus to help us remove the debris we carry from the pain.

Dear Jesus,

I thank you for loving us and bringing forth the emotions we have buried deep inside our hearts. I pray you will touch our broken hearts and will heal them. Thank you for always being at our side. Amen.

Forget about the past

"Brethren, I do not consider that I have made it my own; but one thing I do, forgetting what lies behind and straining forward to what lies ahead, I press on toward the goal for the prize of the upward call of God in Christ Jesus," (Philippians 3:13-14).

Have you dealt with the hurts of your past and still find that at times they can surface? Things you made peace with that still come to the surface when you least expect it and you are surprised at your reaction? Are you running off your feelings?

Personally I had this happen lately, I had something come up that caused my emotions to be stirred. I know I made peace and had let go of this surprise emotion a long time ago so why was it back to prod me?

Perhaps it was a test in faith, to see if my eyes were truly on Jesus. The point is we can either let the negative emotions we have from a hurt fester in us or we can let go and make the decision to leave the past in the past. We need to reflect more on Jesus and His love for us and less on our own pain. There is a time and a place to look at the past but when you know you released that pain and were healed, don't allow unexpected emotions to cause doubt in your heart. We also need to be aware that there is evil and that we need protection from the lies of the enemy. Keep your eyes on Jesus and trust in the good things he has already done in your life and will continue to do for those He loves.

Dear Jesus,

Thank you for loving us and watching over us. I pray for all who are hurting and in need of healing that they will keep their eyes on you and trust in your mercy. That they will believe what you have done for them to be true and not doubt your love for them. Amen.

Do you really love yourself?

"Come to him, to that living stone, rejected by men but in God's sight chosen and precious," (1 Peter 2:4).

Do you believe you are chosen and precious? Do you know how valuable you are? I have to admit I struggle with this from time to time but I am a work in progress. It is hard to believe these words when you have been treated poorly and rejected in society as well as in the presence of your own family. Why do others treat us poorly? And why do we allow and believe their lies? These questions circle my mind when I am in the middle of a situation that allows these feelings of insecurity to surface. My conclusion is that hurting people hurt others, which we know is truth. When you are wounded and feel insecure yourself, things are said or actions are shown that are not truly loving in any way. We allow these negative words to affect us when we don't truly love ourselves or believe we have worth. How do we move forward and truly love and respect ourselves? Start by praying and focusing on Scriptures that speak truth over who you are in Christ and how valuable you truly are. Take it day by day, baby steps of positive talk and over time you can look back and see the progress you are making. It is not easy and we all fall short, but we can change the brokenness if we allow Jesus to heal us.

Dear Jesus,

Thank you for all you are doing in our lives. I pray for all of us who have been hurt by others, and who have allowed the words that cut us deep to fall into our hearts. I pray for healing and for self-confidence for all of us who struggle in this way. Amen.

Search your heart

"O Lord, thou hast searched me and knows me!" (Psalm 139:1).

The Lord knows us even better than we know ourselves, we cannot keep anything from Him. There are times though that our hurts run so deep that we do not even realise that they are hidden in our hearts. We need to pray and ask Jesus to heal our hearts and help us to forgive those who have hurt us. Personally, I had thought I had forgiven someone who hurt me but just recently realised the pain was still there. Hidden pain that up until now first made itself visible to me. How did I deal with this? I asked Jesus to heal my heart of unforgiveness and then through prayer I released this and asked God to bless those who hurt me. This is a process I will continue to do now until I know that the unforgiveness is gone. I was surprised that I was still hanging onto these feelings, but I am also grateful that the Holy Spirit revealed it to me so I could forgive and free myself from that bitterness.

Dear Jesus,

I thank you for loving us and for helping us to grow closer to you. I pray for all who have forgiveness that they can be healed and released from this pain. Heal our broken hearts. Amen.

Put off your old nature

"Put off your old nature which belongs to your former manner of life and is corrupt through deceitful lusts, and be renewed in the spirit of your minds, and put on the new nature, created after the likeness of God in true righteousness and holiness. Therefore, putting away falsehood, let everyone speak the truth with his neighbour, for we are members one of another," (Ephesians 4:22-25).

When I look back at my old self I can surely relate to the first part of this Scripture. I was a very disrespectful and lost person. The world offered me falsehoods, and temporary satisfaction, which I used as an escape from my pain. Being involved in things that were evil just opened up the door for the devil to come into my life, which caused my heart to become hard. I would get angry when people would speak truth and goodness into my life, which made me face my sins. No one knew what I was going through or how I felt, or so I thought.

Then I met Jesus and allowed Him to come into my heart. Slowly He started a work in my heart and my life started to take shape. I began to face the truth and repented of my former ways. Today, I am still a work in progress but I can look back and recognise how far I have come. Truth spoken to us can be painful but it was something I knew I needed to hear. Running away from our problems can never solve them; we need truth to be able to grow in our relationship with Jesus.

Dear Jesus,

Thank you for all you have done in our lives. I pray for those who are afraid to look deep into their hearts and face their pain. I pray for healing for them and ask that the Holy Spirit brings them closer to you. Amen.

Keep your eyes on Christ

"So if you have been raised with Christ, seek the things that are above, where Christ is, seated at the right hand of God. Set your minds on things that are above, not on things that are on earth, for you have died, and your life is hidden with Christ in God. When Christ who is your life is revealed, then you also will be revealed with him in glory," (Colossians 3:1-4).

We all have had moments in our faith walk where we can feel the love of Jesus so closely at times. He blesses us with His love and our faith increases. Have you been challenged to grow in faith soon after? Or to show love in a situation where it seems impossible to break through to someone who does not love you back?

These challenges in life are meant to help us grow. For fruit to take shape in our lives. I have gone through these trials time and time again but I can honestly say I'm getting stronger. My faith is increasing and I'm grateful to God for these circumstances. I have learned to keep my eyes on Jesus and not be distracted as much by what is happening around me. If I focus on the good in my life it can outweigh the bad that is around me. Keep praying and asking Jesus to help you to get past the trials in your life; He will lighten the load and bring you back the peace that could easily be lost.

Dear Jesus,

I thank you for today. I thank you for your love for us and our families. I pray for each one of us who is suffering and hurt to turn to you in our pain. I pray we keep our eyes on you and not be distracted by what is around us. Amen.

Listen to the truth

"In the presence of God and of Christ Jesus, who is to judge the living and the dead, and in view of his appearing and his kingdom, I solemnly urge you: proclaim the message; be persistent whether the time is favourable or unfavourable; convince, rebuke, and encourage, with the utmost patience in teaching. For the time is coming when people will not put up with sound doctrine, but having itching ears, they will accumulate for themselves teachers to suit their own desires, and will turn away from listening to the truth and wander away to myths. As for you, always be sober, endure suffering, do the work of an evangelist, carry out your ministry fully," *(2 Timothy 4:1-5).*

This Scripture is very powerful and packed with truth. In our society today I have seen many new age practices on the rise. People tend to believe in these 'quick fix' misleading occult practices that are causing more pain and draining their pocket books.

I am here to say that the road that leads to Jesus is narrow, and yet so worth travelling. Our society is in such a stage of seeking everything instantly that we forget that good things come to those who wait. We need to strengthen in the virtues of the Holy Spirit which then can lead to true healing of the heart. Let's continue to ask Jesus, especially at Christmas, that we grow in the virtues and our feet stay walking the long, narrow road.

Dear Jesus,

As we come to celebrate your birth, let us ask for strength and wisdom that we follow the Holy Spirit. That all who seek you will find you, and they will have complete trust in you alone. Amen.

Unconditional love

"But when the goodness and loving kindness of God our Saviour appeared, he saved us, not because of any works of righteousness that we had done, but according to his mercy, through the water of rebirth and renewal by the Holy Spirit. This Spirit he poured out on us richly through Jesus Christ, our Saviour, so that, having been justified by his grace, we might become heirs according to the hope of eternal life," (Titus 3:4-7).

Have you ever believed you needed to do well to be loved? That love needs to be earned, not freely given? Why do you think some of us were led to believe that we are worth unconditional love?

Years ago I believed this lie myself. I thought Jesus could never love me for who I am, that I needed to earn His love. My parents never gave me unconditional love, in fact the words 'I love you' were never spoken to me from their mouths. I want you to know that Jesus loves you and it is a genuine love. A love you do not need to earn, a love so pure it can change your heart. Are you willing to trust in that love?

Dear Jesus,

I pray for all those who need an outpouring of your love. That they would recognise that they are your chosen children. That your love need not be earned but it is freely given to those who seek you. Amen.

Don't lose heart

"Consider him who endured such hostility against himself from sinners, so that you may not grow weary or lose heart," (Hebrews 12:3).

There are times in our journey when things go smoothly and times when we are led off track and in different directions. Life is full of ups and downs; we are never exempt from trials.

One thing I am being shown by the Holy Spirit is to keep my eyes on Jesus and not to lose heart. Focus on Jesus and how much He loves us, not on the trials around us. This is hard to do. Yes... we are human, but with the help of the Holy Spirit we can get there. We can start by calling to Jesus for help immediately instead of allowing the things around us to consume our thoughts. Each day start again and reach out to your heavenly Father who is always near His precious children.

Dear Jesus,

I thank you for your love for each of us. Help us to turn to you in trials and to never lose hope. Pour your love over us and give us the grace to know you more each day. Amen.

Lead me Lord

"Answer me quickly, O Lord; my spirit fails. Do not hide your face from me, or I shall be like those who go down to the pit. Let me hear of your steadfast love in the morning, for in you I put my trust. Teach me the way I should go, for to you I lift up my soul. Save me, O Lord, from my enemies; I have fled to you for refuge. Teach me to do your will, for you are my God. Let your good spirit lead me on a level path," (Psalm 143:7-10).

We all want to follow the right path that is pleasing to Jesus. The path that is usually the right path is also the most challenging and difficult one to walk. The bumps and hills on that road can help us to build character and shape us to a deeper love and trust in God. If we turn to Jesus in prayer and careful discernment, He will strengthen us with confirmation that we are on the right path. Place your trust in Him and allow His love to mould you to be the person He created you to be.

Dear Jesus,

I thank you for the bumps and hills in life that have us turn to you for guidance. I pray for continual strength and trust in all of us to seek you wholeheartedly. Thank you for loving us and shaping us. Amen.

Are you on the wrong path?

"When you come into the land that the Lord your God is giving you, you must not learn to imitate the abhorrent practices of those nations. No one shall be found among you who makes a son or daughter pass through fire, or who practices divination, or is a soothsayer, or an augur, or a sorcerer, or one who casts spells, or who consults ghosts or spirits, or who seeks oracles from the dead. For whoever does these things is abhorrent to the Lord; it is because of such abhorrent practices that the Lord your God is driving them out before you. You must remain completely loyal to the Lord your God. Although these nations that you are about to dispossess do give heed to soothsayers and diviners, as for you, the Lord your God does not permit you to do so," (Deuteronomy 18:9-15).

Have you been to a psychic, or have you had your tarot cards read? Have you been involved in reiki, yoga, or any other new age practices that we see today in our society? There are many new age practices popping up in different forms and we need to be very careful in regards to the harm it causes spiritually. I want you to know the devil is real.

In my past I dabbled with psychic phone calls on chat lines, the Ouija board and a few other occult practices. My ignorance led me to become prey to the devil and away from God. I was attracted to the unknown and found these things acceptable in our secular society. Little did I know the harm it caused me spiritually.

To make a long story short, when I turned my life over to Jesus, I had to rebuke all the sins of my past including every new age practice I was involved in. Jesus is the one, true God, He is the long, narrow path that leads us to healing. We need to turn away from sin and find the truth in His loving mercy.

Dear Jesus,

I pray for all who seek healing but have been led down the wrong path. Those who the enemy is grasping at and trying to harm. I ask that they find the truth which is in you alone. Amen.

In His time

"He has made everything beautiful in its time," (Ecclesiastes 3:11).

We all have been hurt and we tend to carry that pain that can affect us spiritually. We are like the hardened bud that needs time to ripen, mature and grow. Inside the bud a beautiful flower is waiting to bloom and radiate its beauty. Only such a process can happen in our lives if we give Jesus the pieces.

If we surrender our pain bit by bit into His hands, He truly will turn that pain into something beautiful. It takes patience and trust for us to truly ripen. Are you willing to allow Him into your pain? Are you willing to be real and honest for growth and change?

Dear Jesus,

I pray for healing for all who are suffering. That they would have trust and allow room for you in their hearts. In your time they will open and bloom. Amen.

Be transformed

"Do not be conformed to this world but be transformed by the renewal of your mind, that you may prove what is the will of God, what is good and acceptable and perfect," (Romans 12:2).

In my garden, I have witnessed the beautiful transformation that takes place when a orchid blooms, a month after appearing to be a mere bud. This transformation speaks to the way God works in our hearts, symbolically. He ripens and prunes us, which leads to a renewal of our minds. When the time is right, and only then, is the true beauty of His work revealed.

We need to be patient and honest with Jesus, revealing the truth of our interior sins. Surrendering the pain and anger allows Him to sculpt the hurt into something beautiful. Beauty that can be used to lead others who suffer to His compassionate and merciful heart. He is waiting patiently for your 'yes', are you willing to allow Him into your heart?

Dear Jesus,

I pray for those who are suffering in silence and who are fearful of opening their hearts to you. I ask that they will trust in your mercy and allow your hand to create beauty in their lives. Amen.

Define love

"It is not rude, it does not see its own interests, it is not quick-tempered, it does not brood over injury," (1 Corinthians 13:5).

What is love? We all most likely refer to love as a squishy, melty feeling. A feeling rather than a decision that we make in regards to how we treat others around us. If we were to only love when our feelings and emotions gave us the go-ahead, how would we grow deeper in relationship to Jesus? How would that be true love?

Let's face it, we all have been wounded, rejected and treated poorly by those around us at one time or another. Our reaction to this might have been ungodly and rather harsh as no one would appreciate being treated poorly. We might have lashed out, which in turn would have caused deeper wounds and sin within our lives as well as on the one who inflicted the pain. How would those actions reflect the love of Christ?

We all are sinners and when we turn our lives over to Jesus we expect Him to accept us as we are. Full of sin, blindness, and deeply hurt by the circumstances that have shaped our lives over time. None of us are perfect and we need to try to look at each other through compassionate eyes. Remembering we expected Jesus to forgive us when we were truly lost without Him.

This does not mean we are to be treated in an abusive way and not allow justice to happen in that regard. What it means is that when we encounter difficulties in our relations with others, we need to look at their hearts and be more compassionate. If we can show love even when we ourselves are hurt and angry by sharp words, we too can be more Christ-like. Step by step as we practise loving with our new eyes of compassion, we can truly show Jesus to our troubled society.

Dear Jesus,

I thank you for loving us and filling our hearts with compassion. I pray for all those who are hurt in our world who need to witness your love in their lives. Touch their hearts and help them to get to know you at a deeper level. Amen.

No one can take your joy

"So you have sorrow now, but I will see you again and your hearts will rejoice, and no one will take your joy from you," (John 16:22).

Have you fallen into despair, self-pity and anger at times? Has the environment around you at work, home or in personal relationships caused you anxiety? I'm guessing many would answer 'yes'. We all have fallen down at times in these situations but have you gotten back up? Were you able to stand and trust in Jesus to take the lead in your struggles?

I felt this way many times and anxiety would suffocate my emotions. Headaches and aches and pains in my body accompanied my mental torments. The truth is I was not allowing Jesus to carry my burdens. What I was saying to Him was 'I do not trust you'.

We need to look closely at ourselves and be real with what is underneath and triggering the response of these emotions. Constant hurts in our lives from others can play a huge part in having trust issues and we need to keep handing over our burdens to the Lord. Step by tiny step, hand Him your worries, cares and frustrations. Be real with Him and speak from your heart when you have trouble trusting and soon you will find the burdens lifting as your trust in Him increases.

Dear Jesus,

I pray for all who struggle in trusting you. I know you can see into their hearts and the areas affecting mistrust in your love for them. I pray for healing in all our lives. Amen.

In thanksgiving

"I will give thanks to the Lord with my whole heart; I will tell of all your wonderful deeds. I will be glad and exult in you; I will sing praise to your name, O most high," (Psalm 9:1-2).

I want you to search your heart and truthfully admit to yourself if you feel blessed. Are you truly grateful for all that you have in your life? Or, do you selfishly feel you deserve more?

These are hard questions that we all need to think about. I have experienced these emotions of feeling upset with failed relationships in regards to not having my biological family love me the way they should. This led me down a path of feeling sorry for myself and wanting something that emotionally was not possible. You can't make people love you, it's not possible.

I overcame this self-pity by looking back at my life and seeing how far I have come. Realising that Jesus loves me and that I needed to love myself. That loving myself was key to how I allowed other people to treat me. I needed to believe that I was valuable and worthy of love.

Today I truly am grateful for all the Lord has done in my life. I will tell of His wonderful deeds and praise His mighty name.

Dear Jesus,

I lift up all the people who are suffering and hurting from a lack of love. People who so desperately need you but have not yet found you. I pray for them to come to know you. You are the only one who can fill their hearts with overflowing love. Amen.

His plan

"For I know the plans I have for you, says the Lord, plans for welfare and not for evil, to give you a future and a hope," (Jeremiah 29:11).

Do you believe God has a plan for you? Do you trust in Him enough to let go and allow His will to be done in your life?

When things are going well it is so easy to say 'yes' to these questions. If you were given some very hard news in your life that upset you, would you allow God to carry your burden? Is it possible to believe He has a plan for you?

My answer today would be 'yes'. I truly do believe and know that He has a plan for you and I. Even offering Him a bit of trust slowly over time due to our own fears pleases Him. He is so willing to walk beside you at your pace. God knows your heart and wants nothing more than to fill you with hope. After all, He created you and has such a special purpose for you to fulfill. Don't feel discouraged when you fall but rather ask for His hand to help you back up.

Dear Jesus,

I thank you for the plan you have for each of our lives. I pray for those who are struggling to know that you truly are with them. In your time, help them to grow in trust and faith. Amen.

A new you

"Remember not the former things, nor consider the things of old. Behold, I am doing a new thing; now it springs forth, do you not perceive it?" (Isaiah 43: 18-19).

Do you keep looking back at your sins even though they were forgiven? Do you truly believe God loves you and wants to restore your life?

I made terrible choices in my life and the consequences were deep-rooted sins that suffocated what was left of my being. Shortly after I turned my life over to Jesus I had to constantly overcome my negative thoughts with His truth. Over and over again I would hear in my mind doubts and fears that shackled me to lies. Did I truly believe I was worthy of love? Did Jesus really forgive me for my sins?

After some time I realised I was forgiven and loved by Jesus, but I did not forgive myself. Not only do we need God's forgiveness but we need to forgive and love ourselves. God looks at our heart, He is compassionate and forgiving. We need to look at ourselves through God's eyes and realise that we are worthy of His love. He truly wants to restore you and do a new thing in your life!

Dear Jesus,

I pray for those who struggle with self-doubt and unforgiveness. I ask that they will come to realise how much you love them and in return will start to love themselves. Amen.

Made whole in His time

"The saying is sure and worthy of full acceptance, that Christ Jesus came into the world to save sinners. And I am the foremost of sinners; but I received mercy for this reason, that in me, as the foremost, Jesus Christ might display his perfect patience for an example to those who were to believe in him for eternal life," (1 Timothy 1:15-16).

This Scripture speaks on how God can change our lives and how merciful He truly is when we turn to Him. Do you know that He died on the cross for your sins? That He loves you so much that He died to save you!

I remember when I started to turn my life around and the thoughts I had running through my mind. I wondered if Jesus loved me or if He had already abandoned me due to my sins. I had committed some big sins and I thought he only loved those who were 'perfect'. Reality is there is no 'perfect' person, it does not exist. We all fall short and are in need of repentance.

Patiently, and in His time He began to heal my brokenness. He will restore your life if you surrender to Him the broken pieces. You need to truly believe in your heart that you are precious and valuable and I know for a fact Jesus looks at the heart. Looking back at past sins will only keep you in the dark and He wants nothing more than to reach those areas with His light. Will you allow

Him to come into your heart and heal the wounds that are keeping you in despair?

Dear Jesus,

I thank you for the love you have for each of us. I thank you for your patience and mercy. I pray for all who feel you are too far from them because of their sins. I ask that they come to believe and realise how much you truly love them. Amen.

Draw near to grace

"Let us then with confidence draw near to the throne of grace, that we may receive mercy and find grace to help in time of need," (Hebrews 4:16).

My 43rd birthday had a significant impact on my train of thoughts. My mother passed away at the same age of a drug overdose. It made me reflect on my own life, being the same age she was when she died so tragically. Thinking about my own children and how this would effect them if they would have been in that situation in their lives. Turning 43, I have to say I feel very much alive and I am grateful Jesus healed me from addiction. I was sinking in my own addictions as a teenager that could have ended differently had I not reached out my hands to God.

I wonder in my mind if my mother would have had a different path if she had known Jesus? Knowing first-hand of His mercy and grace I believe Jesus is with her right now as she looks down from heaven.

It's very hard to lose someone we love. My prayer is for all those trapped in the cycle of addictions to come and open your arms to Christ. Allow Him to come into your life and step by step lead you into His mercy and grace. Draw near to His throne and let His love guide you back to His light.

Dear Jesus,

I pray for all those caught in addiction as well as family members who suffer with them. I ask they come to know you and open their hearts to your love. With your divine guidance I pray their lives will be restored and healed. Amen.

Trust

"Trust in the Lord with all your heart, and do not rely on your own insight. In all your ways acknowledge him, and he will make straight your paths," (Proverbs 3:5-6).

Have you ever had something happen that caused you to become fearful? Did that fear turn to shame which in turn you realised was pride? Let's face it that life has its ups and downs and we have no control over that.

When our stability is shaken it can be very scary. The unknown is something we fear because our control is gone. We no longer hold the 'reins' in our lives. What if we just stopped and took time to quieten our hearts and minds, could you place your trust in God?

If we trust and walk in faith through the unexpected curves and bumps of life, we will come to see something beautiful. I believe we all need to be reminded of the treasure that Jesus has for us and that He would never abandon His beloved children.

Dear Jesus,

I thank you for the ups and downs in our lives. These bumps teach us to place our complete trust in you. I pray you will lead and guide us to follow your will for our lives. Amen.

Grace

"For the grace of God has appeared for the salvation of all men, training us to renounce irreligion and worldly passions, and to live sober, upright, and godly lives in this world, awaiting our blessed hope, the appearing of the glory of our great God and Saviour Jesus Christ, who gave himself for us to redeem us from all iniquity and to purify for himself a people of his own who are zealous for good deeds. Declare these things; exhort and reprove with all authority. Let no one disregard you," (Titus 2:11-15).

The above Scripture reading really struck me as I read it today. We live in a broken world where sin runs rampant, and selfishness has taken root in many lives.

Children grow up in homes where they are free to decide what they want and guidance is non-existent. Addiction of alcohol, drugs and pornography are becoming way too common. Then we have self-help and new age beliefs spiritually harming those in society who innocently fall prey to the doorway of the devil.

I want you to know that even though you feel helpless in some situations, by God's grace you are called to speak truth through this darkness. Keep pressing on and doing what God has called you specifically to do! We need to set good examples for our children and those in society who are hurting. Always look with eyes of compassion and love as you speak truth to those around you.

Dear Jesus,

I thank you for loving us and giving us strength and grace through hard times in our own lives. I pray for those who are severely broken and need your love and mercy. Please heal their hearts and restore them to who you created them to be. Amen.

He will rescue you

"For thus says the Lord God: Behold, I myself will search for my sheep, and will seek them out. As a shepherd seeks out his flock when some of his sheep have been scattered abroad, so will I seek out my sheep; and I will rescue them from all places where they have been scattered on a day of clouds and thick darkness," (Ezekiel 34:11).

The above Scripture speaks so clearly of God's mercy and love for each and every one of us. No one is to be left behind or left out on their own. I can honestly speak from experience that if it was not for God I am not sure I would be here today. My life was a terrible mess of brokenness and despair that had led me down a very dark path.

I reached out in desperation to Jesus at the point that I hit my bottom. I needed to know if God truly existed and if He did, could He actually love me? A very lost person who had sins so deep that I felt consumed in darkness.

Just like in the above Scripture, Jesus was searching for my return to Him. I want you to know that He is always with you and will never leave you. It is us who leave Him. He loves you more than you can ever imagine and He has a special plan for your life. Allow Him to come into your heart and lead you out of your scattered places.

Dear Jesus,

I thank you for everything you have done in my own life and I know you are the Father I never had. I pray you will touch the hearts of those who are suffering and broken, and will restore them to who you intended them to be. Amen.

Call unto Him

"My flesh and my heart may fail, but God is the strength of my heart and my portion forever," (Psalm 73:26).

This picture is of a house plant I have, its branches have grown downwards and then spike up immediately to grasp the sun. It's as though it hits 'rock bottom' before it realises it needs to move towards the light to survive and to flourish.

We all have times in our lives where the weight of trials can pull us down into the darkness. In that darkness we feel weak and discouraged. Our flesh wants us to feel sorry for ourselves and we can fall into self-pity, which, if we let it, could lead us down a very dark, gloomy road.

The above psalm speaks truth about our own weaknesses and trials. Every one of us has fallen and failed at one time or another. You need to remember that no one is perfect and it happens to all of us. The key here is what you allow to happen after you fall. Do you stay on the ground wallowing in your pain? Or do you choose to get back up and wipe the dirt off your body?

Always remember that no matter what you are going through, you are precious to God. He loves you more than you can ever imagine, and He truly is your strength forever!

Dear Jesus,

I thank you for the trials we all have in our lives. It is through those very trials that we can come to realise how much you love us and are with us. Every step in our pain, you are with us holding our hand and giving us strength. Amen.

Sacred Heart of Jesus

"But God shows his love for us in that while we were yet sinners Christ died for us," (Romans 5:8).

Today is the feast day of the Sacred Heart of Jesus. While we reflect on Jesus and His most loving, compassionate heart, allow the above Scripture to sink into your very own heart. Do you even believe or realise how much Jesus loves and cares for you personally?

Jesus died on the cross for you. Even choosing so knowing you were a sinner! His most compassionate heart filled with deep love for you was worth sacrificing His life for your eternal life. It took me a long time to actually believe that Jesus loved me. Why would he want me, a wretched sinner? My self-pity even entertained thoughts of how my own father neglected me and how I should remain rejected.

Stop allowing those emotions of self-pity, rejection, anger or abandonment to keep you blind to the truth. For many years I stayed in bondage trapped in these lies of the devil. Through the Sacraments of the Church and adoration I allowed Jesus to come into my dark, wounded heart. Jesus looks at us with eyes of compassion and wants nothing more than to bring us closer to His most sacred heart.

Dear Jesus,

I thank you for the love you have for each and every one of your children. Through your sacrifice you have rescued those who are hurting and in need of your most compassionate heart. Jesus, we trust in you. Amen.

My stronghold

"The Lord is a stronghold for the oppressed, a stronghold in times of trouble. And those who know thy name put their trust in thee, for thou, O Lord, hast not forsaken those who seek thee," (Psalm 9:9-10).

Have you ever been at a crossroads in your life and desperately cried out to God for direction? While tears stream down your cheeks, you cry out, Lord are you listening?

Personally, I am at a crossroads in my own life and have had numerous fears and doubts creep up into my mind during this time. Battling negative thoughts and emotions can be quite trying and we all need to keep asking Jesus to help us through these hard times. We all have crosses in our lives that each of us has to deal with on a regular basis. Some crosses are very heavy and with the help of Jesus they can become lighter. A few weeks back I went on a walk carrying a huge burden and with tears streaming down my face I looked up into the sky and I saw a cross in the clouds. The above picture gave me strength that particular day to realise that Jesus is with me in my pain. He is our stronghold who truly hears and loves His children.

Dear Jesus,

I pray for those today who are carrying heavy burdens. I

pray that they will release these burdens into your arms for you to touch their hearts and minds. You are the divine physician and healer, whom I pray we all come to know more deeply. Amen.

Total trust

"A man's mind plans his way, but the Lord directs his steps," (Proverbs 16:9).

We all have been placed in difficult situations in our lives where we had to make choices. Depending on the circumstances, these choices most likely would have been made quickly or without much thought. Did you ever stop to consider consulting with God before you made a quick decision out of fear?

I know in the past I made decisions that were done due to my own fears. Acting quickly and not asking my heavenly Father what He wanted me to do. I found myself placed in the same situation a few times due to being impatient and not fully trusting His will. We all have come from different backgrounds and some of the circumstances we have been given can alter how much we can trust others. Walls are put up in our lives to protect us from becoming hurt once again. What if I were to tell you that you truly can trust Jesus, would you believe me?

If you are willing to consult Him I promise you He will never let you down. Yes, you will struggle with trust at first but allow Him to enter your heart. Over time you will see how much He loves you and your trust in Him will grow. Eventually, at your own pace, you will notice how patiently He waited for your love in return. Trust in the Lord to direct your steps and you will walk down the most beautiful path that He created just for you.

Dear Jesus,

I thank you for your love for all of us. I pray for those who need a extra showering of your love that they will find peace and protection through knowing you as Father. Amen.

Pray constantly

"Rejoice always, pray constantly, give thanks in all circumstances; for this is the will of God in Christ Jesus for you," (1 Thessalonians 5:16-18).

Mother Teresa prayed daily, and the joy of the Lord was very evident in her life. The love of Christ flowed from her heart onto all those she had ministered to throughout her life. Do you believe that Jesus wants to do the same in your life? Would you be willing to allow Him into your heart?

Not one of us has a perfect life. We all face trials and difficulties from time to time. The question is how do you react to those difficulties? Do you take your problems directly to Jesus through prayer?

There were times in my life where I hung onto all the problems that came my way. The emotions and frustrations would eat at my mind, and would manifest through my physical wellbeing. Headaches and stomach aches were sure signs that I was not trusting Jesus with my burdens. Eventually, I was able to release these situations into God's hands with full trust in His will for my life. Even the hard stuff I had to deal with has helped me grow in love and compassion for other people. There are still times when I slip and start to carry the heavy loads of life once again but I am quickly reminded to turn to prayer and thanksgiving.

Dear Jesus,

I thank you for my life. I thank you for all the situations that have shaped us to be more loving, kind and compassionate. I pray that we will all turn to you for direction and guidance. Amen.

Count it all joy

"Count it all joy, my brethren, when you meet various trials, for you know that the testing of your faith produces steadfastness," (James 1:2).

Have you ever seen a beautiful flower spring up among weeds? Just like the Scripture found in James, we come to the understanding that trials will indeed test our faith. That testing of faith will produce something beautiful, which will help us to endure all obstacles that come our way.

The hard part is finding joy in these struggles and hurdles we all come across. There are times in my own faith walk when I allowed myself to sit in my own misery. Holding the burden over my own shoulder and having that weight bring me down. Carrying our struggles on our own can cause significant problems, which I know we all can attest to.

What if you were to thank God in advance for His help and grace? Would you be willing to trust Him in advance, even though you are stuck in the weeds?

Dear Jesus,

I thank you for the trials in our lives that have brought us closer to you. I pray for all those who are lost and struggling, that they would praise you in the midst of their storms. Amen.

Uplifting words

"Anxiety in a man's heart weighs him down, but a good word makes him glad," (Proverbs 12:25).

This one sentence of Scripture speaks volumes of truth. Have you ever been down or discouraged? Have you had moments of anxiety or frustration? What if in those moments someone happened to come along who spoke uplifting words to you?

I know that those positive words would help in some way to lighten the load you were carrying. We all have had an experience of how someone speaking love over us has encouraged our lives. I have even seen faces change as well as attitudes when we choose words of love that build up and not tear down.

What if we make it a goal to give one compliment a day to someone in our lives who could use that affirmation? This act of love might be small to you but to the person receiving these words it could mean everything. Your kindness might be the only positivity this person has ever experienced. When we do things out of love we become the hands and feet of Christ that will lead them to gladness and truth.

Dear Jesus,

I thank you for loving each and every one of us. I pray for those who are weighed down with anxiety and depression that they will find peace knowing you as 'Father'. Let us all try to show love to those who are suffering at this time. Amen.

Cleanse yourself

"Since we have these promises, beloved, let us cleanse ourselves from every defilement of body and spirit, and make holiness perfect in fear of God," (2 Corinthians 7:1).

The above Scripture speaks of cleansing ourselves from defilement. Sin separates us from God and if we don't turn to God for forgiveness we will soon lose our way very quickly. Have you had moments of unconfessed sin that led you further and further away from God?

Before I knew God I lived a very sinful life. I was raised in a dysfunctional home and through my brokenness I became reckless. I got involved in occult things and soon turned to drugs and alcohol to soothe my pain. Jail time, divorce, adultery and abortion were all sins that defiled me. I was lost and emerged in darkness. The devil was active in my life and made his presence known to me.

After many years of suffering in my own misery I turned to Jesus. Desperately, I cried out to Him and He responded. I sat in the confessional for a very long time emptying the garbage that consumed me. I thank Jesus each day for His love and mercy that He poured out into my heart. Do you know that He loves you and wants to do the same for you?

Dear Jesus,

I love you so very much and I pray that others will turn to you for forgiveness. I pray that they will find the love and peace in their own lives that only you can provide. Amen.

Our merciful God

"Come now let us reason together, says the Lord: though your sins are like scarlet, they shall be white as snow; though they are red like crimson, they shall become like wool," (Isaiah 1:18).

This picture was taken when I was a guest at EWTN. It is a memorial for the unborn and in the picture you can see the radiant light that is cast down over the site. The reality of our society is to discard life, and sadly we don't even value how sacred it really is. We have fallen due to our own selfish ways in which our sins have become red like crimson.

Abortion removes a life that will never be. It takes a life and causes regret to those who choose it. My past choice of abortion had me shackled to shame, guilt and unforgiveness for many years. Many men and women suffer in silence from abortion and are in need of God's love and mercy. Are you willing to seek help and forgiveness? Will you open the door of your heart to Jesus?

Breaking my own silence from my past was crucial in being set free. It released the shackles of guilt and shame that tormented my mind. Start by opening up to someone you trust and ask the Holy Spirit to lead you to the right places where you can find healing. You are not alone and in time you will be made white as snow.

Dear Jesus,

I pray for those who are suffering in silence, that they will find hope and healing. That fear and shame will not hold them captive any longer, and they too will find forgiveness. Amen.

Mould us Father

"Yet, O Lord, thou art our Father; we are the clay, and thou art our potter; we are all the work of thy hand," (Isaiah 64:8).

The above Scripture gives us an image of how God can shape our lives just as a sculptor shapes clay. The Lord is the potter who sculpts and shapes our hearts and gives our lives structure. We are all moulded and hand-picked for a purpose and a plan. Are you willing to allow God to shape your life, to smooth out the cracks?

Surrendering pain and trauma is not easy to do especially when it is all we know. Broken, shattered and cracked we show these visible scars which have damaged our own self-worth and image. What if I told you those cracks could be filled and restored, would you believe me? Do you know that those shattered broken pieces could become something beautiful?

If we allow God to come into our hearts He can restore what was broken. The restored pieces we were once ashamed of can help other people who have the same cracks in their lives. Personally, I am so blessed to be able to look at my own life and visibly see the progress of restoration. What God has done in my life, He wants to also do through you, His beautiful vessel.

Dear Jesus,

I pray for all those who feel broken and damaged. I ask that they will come to know God as their Father. That they would open their hearts to His everlasting love. Amen.

Truth

"The grass withers, the flower fades; but the word of our God will stand for ever," (Isaiah 40:8).

This picture shows the beauty of a particular flower that had just blossomed. Within a few days the flower will shrink and slowly fall off, toppling to the ground. The beautiful flower soon fades away and becomes a memory.

Throughout our lives we experience many different changes and circumstances. They can be within our own relationships, friendships and families. The various challenges we face also wither and fade over time, continuing into a endless cycle. Craving stability in your life seems far-fetched. Does this sound familiar?

The word of God will never change. Reading the truth in the Scriptures will bring stability into your life. You will soon begin to find solace and peace in the unfading truth of God. Allow God's love to speak to your heart as you find shelter in his words.

Dear Jesus,

I pray for all those who are suffering in silence, that they will turn to you for comfort. I pray they will find true peace and love that only you can provide. Amen.

New every morning

"The steadfast love of the Lord never ceases, his mercies never come to an end; they are new every morning; great is thy faithfulness," (Lamentations 3:22-23).

The morning sunrise reminds me how each day is a gift from God. Each day is a treasure and God waits patiently for us to recognise that. Do you believe each day is a precious gift?

When you face difficulties and it seems like there is no way out, I want you to know Jesus is with you.

When you feel alone and scared, I want you to know Jesus is with you. When you struggle with lack of faith, I want you to know Jesus is with you.

In the morning as you witness the sunrise, allow God to speak to your heart as He shares that beautiful moment with you alone. You are His beloved child and His love for you is everlasting.

Dear Jesus,

Thank you for each day that you have given us. I pray for those who feel lost and helpless, that they would recognise your mercy and love for them. That they would find comfort and healing as they draw closer to you. Amen.

Divine peace

"I have said this to you, that in me you may have peace. In the world you have tribulation; but be of good cheer, I have overcome the world," (John 16:33).

Recently I have had my fair share of trials. Struggling with the unknown of certain circumstances and waiting to see how things were going to unfold. As I faced one serious trial I soon had several other obstacles placed on my path. The weight and stress of it all soon became a very heavy burden and I asked my heavenly Father to help me.

I was feeling very overwhelmed and I knew that I needed to stay close to God, which gave me peace through the storm. In the past I used to carry my own burdens, which would cause anxiety and physical ailments. It took a while before I could trust Jesus and He waited patiently with me. I am grateful now that I have Jesus in my life and that He has given me the gift of faith. I want you to know that Jesus loves you very much and He is always with you. Turn to prayer and adoration when you are heavily burdened and seek the peace that can only come through Him.

Dear Jesus,

I thank you for the gift of faith. I pray that each one of us that calls on your name will receive this special gift. It is through faith that our eyes will be open and our hearts will be healed. Amen.

Prince of Peace

"For to us a child is born, to us a son is given; and the government will be upon his shoulder, and his name will be called Wonderful Counsellor, Mighty God, Everlasting Father, Prince of Peace," (Isaiah 9:6).

The above Scripture is ideal to reflect upon at Christmas. Wonderful Counsellor, Mighty God, Everlasting Father, Prince of Peace, are ways to describe the precious gift that Jesus is to each and every one of us. The birth of our Lord and Saviour is the ultimate gift of love and peace that our world so desperately needs.

Each Christmas I hope and pray that many people will turn their lives over to Christ and allow Him to heal their brokenness. Allow Jesus to fill you with His peace and love that only He can provide. The true peace that surpasses all understanding.

The Prince of Peace is waiting for your 'yes' to enter your heart at Christmas. Will you give Jesus your 'yes'?

Dear Jesus,

I pray specifically for those who are suffering and alone at Christmas, that they will come to know you as their heavenly Father. That your love for them will melt away all their anxiety, and peace will fill their hearts. Amen.

Pray

"But I say to you that hear: Love your enemies, do good to those who hate you, bless those who curse you, pray for those who abuse you," (Luke 6:27-28).

In the above Scripture Jesus is asking us to forgive and pray for those who have mistreated us. This can be a very tall order to follow, especially when you have been hurt deeply by those who were supposed to protect you. When the pain is so deep and raw how is this even possible?

This is a Scripture we all need to work on each and every day throughout our entire lives. Let's face it, life is not easy and we will always encounter people in our lives who are hurting. The old saying rings true that 'hurt people hurt others'. When our hearts are full of anger and unforgiveness, where do we start?

It starts with you. If you are waiting for the other person to say sorry first, you might be waiting a very long time. You need to turn that hurt over to Jesus and allow Him to work in both of your hearts. It will not be easy at first to pray for someone who hurt you so deeply, but I promise with small steps you will not regret forgiving and releasing that pain. Over time you will be amazed as to what Jesus has done. Are you ready to forgive?

Dear Jesus,

I thank you for the love you have for each and every one of us. I pray especially for those who have unforgiveness, that they would be able to forgive and be set free. I ask that you would heal their hearts and minds. Amen.

Praise

"Praise the Lord! Praise, O servants of the Lord, praise the name of the Lord! Blessed be the name of the Lord from this time forth and for evermore! From the rising of the sun to its setting the name of the Lord is to be praised! The Lord is high above all nations and his glory above the heavens!" (Psalm 113:1-40).

There are so many things we should appreciate and be grateful for within our lives. The sad thing is many people are blind to the blessings that surround them. Have you not recognised the blessings the Lord has given you?

There are so many things we take for granted in our fast-paced society. The beauty of nature can be overlooked and we become deaf to God's still voice that is calling us closer to Him. Have you forgotten that He created you, His most precious child?

Take time to reflect on all the blessings Jesus has given you throughout your life. Spend time in prayer and thank Him for all He has done. Sing songs of thanksgiving and allow Him into your heart as you praise His mighty name! Praise the name of the Lord! The Lord of all creation!

Dear Jesus,

I thank you for all that you have done for us. I thank you for each and every blessing. We are grateful for everything you have provided us with each and every day. Amen.

Do not be anxious

"Therefore I tell you, do not be anxious about your life, what you shall eat or drink, nor about your body, what you shall put on. Is not life more than food, and the body more than clothing? Look at the birds of the air; they neither sow nor reap nor gather into barns, and yet your heavenly Father feeds them. Are you not of more value than they?" (Matthew 6:25-26).

The above Scripture speaks about trusting God to care and provide for our needs. We are called to trust God and not to be anxious when we struggle to make ends meet. This is extremely hard to do especially when our income barely covers our basic needs. Can you relate?

One particular year was very trying for my family and I. As a family, we had to live each day holding on to the promise of this Scripture. Learning to trust God deeply with our financial needs and to truly believe He would provide for us.

Personally, my trust in Him increased during this time, and I can honestly say I was not anxious. When I look back at my past struggles I can recognse how God provided. During every hardship and setback He was with me to hold me up and pull me through. Do you believe He wants to do the same for you?

I want you to know that Jesus loves you, and that He cares about every detail in your life. Have a conversation with Him in prayer and reveal what makes you anxious in your life right now. Be real and honest as you strengthen your trust in Him.

Dear Jesus,

I thank you for today. I thank you for the gift of life and for loving us, your children. I pray that in our difficult situations we can place our trust in you. Amen.

Why are you afraid?

"And when he got into the boat, his disciples followed him. And behold, there arose a great storm on the sea, so that the boat was being swamped by the waves; but he was asleep. And they went and woke him, saying, 'Save us Lord, we are perishing'. And he said to them, 'Why are you afraid, O men of little faith?' Then he rose and rebuked the winds and the sea; and there was a great calm. And the men marvelled, saying, 'What sort of man is this, that even wind and sea obey him?' (Matthew 8:23-27).

The above Scripture speaks well of our own mistrust and fears. The apostles feared they would drown and die, as the storm shook the boat with intense waves. Even though they walked beside Jesus and knew He was the son of God, they were fearful. Is it hard to trust? What do you fear?

We all have our own fears that can hold us back. Fear that can cripple us spiritually, mentally and physically. Fear can lead us down a dark path of despair if we allow it to control us. How can we start to trust and believe Jesus is with us?

You start with taking one step at a time. If we have been deeply wounded in areas of trust in our own lives we can become fearful of others. We place walls around us and not allowing anyone in to prevent the possibility of becoming hurt again. Be patient with yourself and ask Jesus to help you.

He loves you very much and He knows you more than anyone else in the entire world. As you start to trust Jesus, He will calm the storm in your life and your fears will slowly melt away. Be patient with yourself as you grow in relationship with your heavenly Father.

Dear Jesus,

I thank you for all the blessings in our lives, and for always being with us. I pray for all those who are broken and lost, that they will trust in you for comfort and healing. Thank you for your protection and love for each and every one of your children. Amen.

Peace

"Have no anxiety about anything, but in everything by prayer and supplication with thanksgiving let your requests be made known to God. And the peace of God, which passes all understanding, will keep your hearts and your minds in Christ Jesus," (Philippians 4:6-7).

When I reflect upon the magnificence of the sunrise, I am reassured that God created everything including you and I, and that He is very much in control. I also gain a sense of peace, which comes from our Heavenly Father. Do you hear God speak to your heart in the still, quiet moments?

If you feel restless inside, do you speak to God about your feelings or do you bury them within? Do you take time each day and pray about the situations that cause you anxiety? Will you open your heart and allow Jesus to fill you with peace that only He can provide?

Start by taking small steps in prayer each day and read the words of Jesus from your Bible. As you turn to Jesus in prayer He will comfort your anxious mind.

Over time your trust in Him will increase as you begin to develop a relationship with your Father. The peace only Jesus can provide will soon flood your heart and mind as you turn to Him in prayer.

Dear Jesus,

I pray for those who are sick and suffering and in need of your healing. I also pray for trust and peace for all who are troubled and anxious. Fill us with your love and peace as we turn to you in prayer. Amen.

Jesus died for you

"But God shows his love for us in that while we were yet sinners Christ died for us," (Romans 5:8).

We all fall short and are sinners, but yet Jesus died for us. He died on the cross to atone for our sins, and to give us eternal life in heaven, even knowing we would fall. Jesus suffered immensely because of His deep, compassionate love for us all. Are you truly aware of how much He loves you?

When I reflect on my own life prior to having a relationship with God, I have to admit I was deeply consumed in sin. Drowning in darkness and despair was all I knew and my choices reflected that. I questioned if God could even love or want someone like myself that had one foot in the pit of hell. The question of whether I was even worthy of His love was commonly echoed throughout my mind and heart.

As I reached out to Jesus in prayer I soon realised that He truly loves me, a broken sinner. In fact, He died on the cross carrying our burdens and sufferings. What He has done in my life has transformed the darkness into light. Jesus wants to do the same in your life and He is waiting patiently for you to open up your heart to Him. Are you willing to let go and let God fill you with His peace and love?

Dear Jesus,

I pray for all the people who are consumed in darkness and can't find the light. I pray for their conversions and that they would find the peace and love that only you can provide. I thank you for dying on the cross for me a sinner. I love you so very much. Amen.

Be still

"Be still, and know that I am God. I am exalted among the nations, I am exalted in the earth!" (Psalm 46:10).

During the 2020 coronavirus pandemic, my family and I were unable to attend Mass for more than two months. The emotion I had after I received Holy Communion for the first time upon our return to Mass was a true grace from God. The peaceful silence I so craved whispered 'be still' to my mind as I rested in that moment. It was hard to leave church not knowing when I would be able to come back again.

In life, we face many uncertainties but we must not lose hope. Staying close to Jesus in His written word and through prayer can offer that hope. Building a relationship with Jesus takes time, and now we are given that time. Are you willing to make time for Jesus?

Start each day with praising and thanking God. Personally, I am thankful for the flowers that are blooming in my garden. There are lots of things to be thankful for and we need to appreciate the gifts around us. If we slow down and be still, that is where we will find God.

Dear Jesus,
I thank you for the gift of today. I pray for all those who have

lost hope and are discouraged, that they would turn to you for consultation. I pray that they would be filled with the peace and joy that only comes from you. Amen.

Purify your heart

"Draw near to God and he will draw near to you. Cleanse your hands, you sinners, and purify your hearts, you men of double mind," (James 4:8).

The second sentence from this specific Scripture challenges us to look into our own hearts. In all honesty this is a very hard thing to do, as pride can detour this truth. Many people have trouble facing their sins and find it easier to just bury them deep within. Have you personally done the same in your life? Have you buried the pain?

The truth is that we need to be honest and real with God in order to grow fruit in our lives. That sin you are hiding is not hidden from God's eyes, and he can't be fooled. We need to look deep within our own hearts and repent of the sins we have committed. I have learned that as hard as it is I personally need to reflect daily on my own sins and weaknesses to grow in a personal relationship with Jesus. Are you ready to grow closer to Jesus in your life?

Jesus is waiting for you to draw closer to Him. Let us purify our hearts as we call out to Jesus for forgiveness and mercy. Are you ready to repent from the sins that have shackled you?

Dear Jesus,

I thank you for this time you have given us to grow closer to you. I pray for all those who are lost and afraid to turn to you for comfort and healing. Amen.

Prayer

"Rejoice in your hope, be patient in tribulation, be constant in prayer," (Romans 12:12).

Mother Teresa is one of my favourite saints. Her life was devoted to prayer and it was reflected in the fruits of her work. Love and joy radiated throughout her as she cared for those most in need. Prayer was significant in Mother Teresa's life and there are many articles and books where you can read and learn more about her beautiful story. How often do you pray yourself? Do you believe in the power of prayer?

Many people struggle with prayer and find it hard to start a conversation with Jesus. It can be difficult at first but if you give Jesus a few minutes a day in prayer, you won't regret it. I personally love talking to Jesus and sharing with Him the deepest secrets within my heart. I always feel so much better after a good cry when I confidently share my heart with my Father. Jesus wants a personal relationship with you, are you willing to spend some time with Him?

Dear Jesus,

I thank you for today and all that you have provided for us. I pray for those who are struggling with their prayer life that they will make the time to share their hearts with you. Amen.

Come to me

"Come to me, all who labour and are heavy laden, and I will give you rest," (Matthew 11:28).

In June each year, Catholics celebrate the Feast of the Sacred Heart of Jesus. The symbol of Jesus' heart represents His passionate love for us. The reason I chose this particular Scripture for this reflection is because it speaks volumes on Jesus' invitation to rest in His love.

There are many people who are feeling burdened and stressed over the events taking place around us. Worries, doubts, and the fear of the unknown burden the minds and hearts of many. Financial concerns are very real, which can cause extra weight on your already heavy shoulders. What if I told you I knew where you could release the heavy baggage you're carrying, would you listen?

The answer is Jesus. Jesus is waiting patiently for you with His arms stretched out to comfort you. Believe in His love for you and I assure you, you will find the rest you desire. Are you willing to rest in His love?

Dear Jesus,

I thank you for the love you have for each of us. I pray for those who have worries, doubts and fears and are suffering at this time. I pray that they would turn to your Sacred Heart for consolation and healing. Amen.

Like a child

"Cast all your anxieties on him, for he cares about you," (1 Peter 5:7).

This picture shows a child in a conversation with Jesus or perhaps just being comforted in His presence. I absolutely love this image and the reflection it has on our own personal relationship with Jesus.  Do you know that Jesus cares about you deeply and wants a personal relationship with you?

We all have challenges and hardships in our lives and the weight of that can really be heavy. Some challenges are like boulders, while others can be as light as a pebble. No one is free from facing problems within their lives and it is how we deal with the burden that will make the load lighter. Would you open your heart to Jesus like this child in the picture, and trust in His love for you?

When I am faced with problems I find it so comforting to share my heart with Jesus. Over the years I have learned that if I run to my heavenly

Father like a child, He is there waiting with open arms. He loves and cares for you deeply and is wanting you to speak to Him. The next time you feel the weight of the world on your shoulders, will you turn to Jesus?

Dear Jesus,

I thank you for the love you have for us, your children. I pray for all those who are carrying heavy burdens to place them at the foot of the cross. I ask that they would be comforted by your Fatherly love for them. Amen.

Peace

"Peace I leave with you; my peace I give to you; not as the world gives do I give to you. Let not your hearts be troubled, neither let them be afraid," (John 14:27).

This picture was taken last year in Newfoundland where we travelled for our vacation. I find the sounds of the ocean water touching the shore very calming and peaceful. Stepping into a place with such beauty can easily allow us to forget the troubles of this world. For myself, I find it very relaxing and liberating to slow down and take time in silence to allow Jesus to speak to my heart.

We are surrounded by constant noise and distractions in our everyday life which makes it hard to hear the Holy Spirit. The hustle and bustle of busyness has sadly become first priority in so many people's lives. Peace has been replaced with anxiety, fear and division. Have you personally lost peace in your own life? Are you willing to spend some time with Jesus?

Looking back in my own life I would allow fear and anxiety to consume me to the point where I was affected physically. The symptoms which stemmed from that caused numerous stomach aches and headaches. It was only through spending time with Jesus and building trust in Him that I was freed from my physical ailments. As I started to trust Jesus, my fear and anxiety were replaced with peace. Through spending time with Jesus I have grown to love silence and the peace that accompanies it. Only Jesus can provide true peace that lasts forever.

Dear Jesus,

I pray for those who are anxious and restless. I ask that they will seek peace that only comes from a personal relationship with you. I pray for the conversion of hearts who are lost and misguided, that they will turn to you their heavenly Father. Amen.

Praise His name

"From the rising of the sun to its setting the name of the Lord is to be praised!" (Psalm 113:3).

One particular morning I was blessed to catch the sunrise as I opened up my blinds. The beauty of the sunrise once again reminded me to appreciate the moment and to see the good in each day. When we overlook the beauty around us, we tend to close our hearts and ears to God's still, small voice.

Do you take time in your day to appreciate all the blessings you have?

We can forget the blessings we have been given most easily when we are going through trials in our lives. Hardships can blind us at times to the hope that is found only through Jesus Christ. Jesus is always with us and sometimes we need to be reminded of that. Are you willing to open your heart to Jesus?

Each day take the time to recognise the sunsets in your life that are blessings from God. Praise the name of Jesus through music and prayer as you turn to thank the Lord for all the good things He has done for you. Tomorrow when you open up your blinds allow your heart to see the beauty that surrounds you.

Dear Jesus,

I thank you for today and all the beauty that surrounds us. I thank you for the gift of life and all you have created. Thank you Lord for the blessings in our lives. Amen.

Strength

"My flesh and my heart may fail, but God is the strength of my heart and my portion forever," (Psalm 73:26).

Once, on a morning walk I noticed the beautiful red sun above a rugged staircase. I stopped and took a photo as the picture reflected my own journey with Christ. There are days which seem smooth like the bottom stairs and then we have times that are challenging and rough which reflect the upper stairs. It is a good reminder of how much we need Jesus in our lives to help us through our rugged staircases.

There are also times where we are made aware of our own character traits that we see as smooth, but which are in fact more rough and rocky. The Holy Spirit will remove the scales from our eyes and reveal to us where we need to grow, if we humbly turn to Jesus in prayer. We all fall short and are in need of God's grace and mercy that comes from asking His forgiveness for our sins. With strength that comes only through Jesus we can endure the stairs that are set before us.

Dear Jesus,

Thank you for the trials in our lives that bring us closer to you. Through these struggles I ask that we will grow in trust and patience as we turn to you for strength. Thank you for your everlasting love for each and every one of your children. Amen.

Bless the Lord

"I will bless the Lord at all times; his praise shall continually be in my mouth. My soul makes its boast in the Lord; let the afflicted hear and be glad. O magnify the Lord with me, and let us exalt his name together!" (Psalm 34:1-3).

There are days that can be extremely difficult and we can quite easily become discouraged and frustrated. Times where we feel lost and our minds become filled with unanswered questions. The thoughts that run through your mind could lead to anxiety and fear in a matter of minutes. Are you willing to seek Jesus in the midst of your trial?

Instead of allowing fear to consume your mind, turn to Jesus who is always at the door of your heart. If we turn our fear into praise, the Prince of Peace will fill our hearts with love and joy. Jesus can heal our hearts and bring true peace in the midst of our storms. Together let us exalt His name as we praise our king!

Dear Jesus,

I thank you for the trials that bring us closer to you. Help us to trust in you more each and every day. With thanksgiving and praise we turn to you in search of true peace and restoration. Amen.

The light shines in the darkness

"The light shines in the darkness, and the darkness has not overcome it," (John 1:5).

Recently I stumbled upon article after article on the darkness that is around us, and I can see how people are feeling lost and hopeless. The constant negative headlines can be very overwhelming for a lot of people and the overdose and suicide rates have been sky-rocketing. Hearing the news of so many young people dying of overdoses weighs so heavily on my heart, as I lost my mother to an overdose when I was a teenager. My mother's death impacted me so much, and opened my eyes to the darkness of drugs, which stole away a precious life.

I personally went down the dark road of addiction as well, but witnessing the death of my mother woke me up. My mother saved my life by waking me up to the realisation that addictions can kill you. Ignorantly as a young teen I thought I was invincible and that my body could easily rebound from the abuse I was putting it through. Obviously this is not reality and the darkness of addiction is real. Are you sick of being a prisoner to your addictions?

I want you to know that there is hope and that you are precious to God. Jesus loves you so very much and wants you to turn to Him in the midst of your pain and suffering. You are so valuable and loved. Jesus has a unique plan for your life and wants you to know how special you are to Him. The light shines in the darkness, and the darkness has not overcome it.

Dear Jesus,

I thank you for bringing me out of darkness and into your glorious light. I pray especially for those who are lost in addictions that they too will find hope and healing. Help them to see how precious and loved they truly are. Amen.

Hope

"May the God of hope fill you with all joy and peace in believing, so that by the power of the Holy Spirit you may abound in hope," (Romans 15:13).

It can be easy to become discouraged if we allow the negative talk we hear to decide our emotions. We can choose to look only at the bad that is happening, which most often leads us to become frustrated and angry. With this choice all hope we once had is quickly lost and forgotten as negativity dwells in our hearts. Are you feeling hopeless right now?

Think back to the times when God made His presence known to you, and rest in the love that He has for you. In these moments that seem hopeless, it helps to remember the struggles we have overcome in our own personal lives, and to reflect on how Jesus pulled us through those challenges. When I encounter hardships it helps me significantly to reflect back on all the times that Jesus was with me through the storms. Knowing that when I turn to Jesus in prayer it leads to a deep peace and hope that can only come through Him. Each day spend some time with Jesus and allow the peace of the Holy Spirit to rest in your heart.

Dear Jesus,

I thank you for all the times that you have rescued me throughout my life. You brought me out of darkness and into your light. I pray for all those who are lost and in darkness that they too will come to know your love for them. Amen.

www.ingramcontent.com/pod-product-compliance
Lightning Source LLC
Chambersburg PA
CBHW051358290426
44108CB00015B/2069